SURREAL ESTATE

13 Canadian poets under the influence

SURREAL ESTATE

13 Canadian poets under the influence

edited by stuart ross

THE MERCURY PRESS

The publisher gratefully acknowledges the financial assistance of the Canada Council for the Arts, the Ontario Arts Council, the Ontario Book Publishing Tax Credit Program, and the Ontario Media Development Corporation. The publisher further acknowledges the financial support of the Government of Canada through the Department of Canadian Heritage's Book Publishing Industry Development Program (BPIDP) for our publishing activities.

Editor for the press: Beverley Daurio
Cover design: Bill Kennedy
Cover photograph: Pamela Stewart
Composition and page design: Beverley Daurio
Proofreading: Beverley Daurio and Angela Rawlings
Helper: Tyler Daurio

Printed and bound in Canada
Printed on acid-free paper

1 2 3 4 5   08 07 06 05 04

Canadian Cataloguing in Publication Data

Ross, Stuart
Surreal estate: 13 Canadian poets under the influence

ISBN 1-55128-109-0
I. Title II. Series
PS8576.I32S97 2001   C811'.54   C2001-902999-3
PR9199.3.M4564S97 2001

The Mercury Press
Box 672, Station P,
Toronto, Ontario Canada M4S 2Y4
www.themercurypress.ca

CONTENTS

INTRODUCTION

This isn't a book of Surrealist poetry, nor a book of poetry by Surrealists (although at least a couple of the contributors would label themselves thusly). *Surreal Estate* pulls together a small but wildly varied community of writers whose work — either directly or via various literary detours — has been influenced by the literary phenomenon spearheaded by Breton, Jacob, Eluard, Reverdy & Co. from 1924 until the second world war.

Surrealism's precursor, Dada, was an assault on both Western art and on human savagery. More broadly, it was assault on sense. Surrealism grew out of Dada's rubble, taking on European political and artistic rationalism by endeavouring to excavate truths through rejecting reason and embracing fantasy and dream states. Similarly, the ribbons of Surrealism streaming through the underground — and occasionally the mainstream (if such a term can be applied to something as marginal as poetry) — of Canadian literature are a product of artists dedicated to the transmutation of the written word and, in some cases, of North American society itself.

The poets in this book may never be part of any recognized canon in a country where including the word "surreal" on the jacket copy of a poetry book is punishable by death. Or perhaps just banishment from university reading lists. But they are among the most active poets in Canada — publishing in the micropresses and the trade houses, making experimental and punk music, operating their own imprints, magazines, record labels, and websites, creating visual art, and, in a couple of cases, even launching their own art movements.

When I first conceived of this book, I imagined "post-Surrealist" would appear somewhere on the cover. Just as the punk rock movement was a product of working-class England in the late 1970s, when disco and

AOR dominated the airwaves, I felt that true Surrealism was specific to Europe between the wars. But a couple of the poets I wanted to include took issue: they were Surrealists, they said, no "post" about it. (Not that I'd complain if this anthology contributed to the destruction of Western capitalism!) I'd guess that at least a couple of the other potential contributors were surprised that their work would be "surreal enough" for such a collection.

Such is the range of this small anthology: there are those here who feel they are writing a pure Surrealism, and even live the philosophy, and others who absorbed their surreal content through other sources: the Burroughs wing of the Beats, magic realism, Language poetry, the New York Poets, and neo-surrealists and absurdists like Joe Rosenblatt and Opal Louis Nations.

I have a sneaking suspicion that one big reason surrealist writing is taboo is because humour is taboo. If you're being funny, you can't be a serious poet. You can't be worth studying in university. But also, we live in a society that respects control, power, and conscious decision (to invade sovereign countries, destroy natural environments, guzzle natural resources, etc.). Those of us who embrace the possibilities of randomness, absurdism, chance, error, and the unconscious are happily out of step.

There are more than a handful of poets in North America who have been heavily influenced by Surrealism. Some even consider themselves Surrealists, employing automatism among their writing methods, while others carry trace elements of the movement. They might read Benjamin Peret and Max Jacob, or they might dream profusely. Maybe they write while they writhe with fever, after smoking some grass, or while banging their heads against their desktops. Maybe they're just weird.

This anthology brings together thirteen Canadian poets under the influence of Surrealism. As it turns out, I know everyone in this book, and many of them know each other. Most were born in the 1960s, and at least one in the early 1970s. I was born in 1959. The poets here are mainly Toronto-based — and the ones who live in Hamilton, Wolfville,

First South, and Vancouver have also spent formative writing years in Toronto. I don't believe that Toronto is a subversive nest of Surrealism, but perhaps the joke of capitalism's façade of order is most apparent in this sprawling urban/suburban nexus.

These thirteen writers show that the force of Surrealism is still strong, more than three-quarters of a century after it was hatched by Apollinaire and Breton, and it manifests itself in a startling range of ways. There are lyric poems here, and Language poems. Prose poems and manifestos. Narrative poems and list poems. Things that could just about be called haiku. I've included a generous selection of work from each of the writers, most of it previously unpublished. In the back of the book you'll find a round table of the poets' bios and artistic statements, in their own words.

Any such introduction must, it seems, include the following: this anthology doesn't claim to be complete. An earlier generation of Canadian poets was also heavily influenced by Surrealism: Rosenblatt, bill bissett, David McFadden, bpNichol, Victor Coleman, and others. Surrealism also laces the work of several Canada-U.S. border-crossers: Mark Strand, Anne Carson, Robert Sward, and continent-hopper Nations. And, during the production of this book, I've stumbled upon enough interesting younger writers to construct a *Surreal Estate II*.

Doubtless there are many other agents of dream reality and practitioners of chance out there, many not even recognizing themselves as such. Their infiltration is essential to keeping Canadian poetry on its toes — and interesting.

Stuart Ross
Toronto, 2004

Gil Adamson

LITTLE BLACK HATS

The beautiful women are
kissing one another
bending forward in cafés
knocking fences over
ignoring the law of gravity
and floating
in tailored suits.

One woman appears
to the entire city at rush hour
big as a cloud
spawning fistfights
a rise in shoplifting
as clerks gaze upward.
Men rush from boarding houses
their dogs yapping
comb-overs flying up.
They are appalled, and say so.

The press asks Audrey Hepburn
why everyone looks like her.
She smiles, begins to float.
I'm as baffled, she says,
as you are.
We all nod her head.

The press attacks other things.
Like a dog with too many sticks
it rushes away.
Audrey sits in the shade

opens her purse, stares into it.
All the movies, the dresses
all those worries about age
and now look, she thinks
rising through parade streamers
as the music begins
closing her eyes
dreaming of one kind word.

THE JUDGE

I've lost my suitcase
in the dark woods.
Apes are taking it apart
knuckling through my panties
sniffing my truckers' magazines.
One of them puts the flashlight
in his mouth, snaps it on
and his head lights up red.
The rest of them scatter
leaving him alone
with me, my life around him
his mouth a shadowy red theatre.
I watch the curious tongue moving.
A blind thing, telling my fortune.

DEAR BOTH:

Thanks for the cup of sugar.
But now I have lost receipts
photocopies, keys.
My paint is peeling
the kettle boiling itself hoarse
and I stand in my kitchen
hands over my ears.

On Tuesday, a crowd of little boys
manoeuvred me into an alley
tugboats nudging the Queen Mary
and squeezed me hard against a wall.
Oh, those tiny digging fingers!
But they were just practising
and I'm always glad to help; boys
need education, after all.

Alone in my apartment, however
I can't find my father.
And all across the walls
those shadows of my mother.
At least it looks like her shape.
And that other one, his head
under a black hood
saying "Look at the birdie!"
the one snapping the pictures;
white hot outlines
of my mother, running.

Apart from that, yes. I'm fine.

Little things come up my drains.
Little black dots

that swarm and breed
and congregate round my bed
at night, singing.
Happy, happy
they laugh at my jokes
honk their horns
and race along the corduroy roads
of my hardwood floor.

O, dear both
sometime when you're free
I'll invite a few people over
to see.
We'll sit in my bed
thigh to thigh
looking down east to the drive-in
or up west to the black dot café.
We'll eat popcorn, turn out the lights
and maybe, out in the fields
near my crumpled nylons
we'll see two dots burying a third
beside an idling car.

There are so many things
I'd like to show you.
Perhaps an itinerary of
my father's trip to gone
or my own hopes
creeping into cupboards
knocking over cans of soup.

I'd like to have your apartment
if you don't mind
and you can have mine.
Think of it!
All the nightly entertainment
and the lovely outlines
flashing down the hall;
my mother, panicking again
taking the paint with her.

I'm just not working out —
please don't blame yourselves.
My mother always said I was shallow.
She said: Sure, good things come to you
but look how small they are.

VAPOUR TRAIL

"If I had a choice, I'd take more fuel."
— *Neil Armstrong*

A rocket comes
promising a dent in time.

It says: I am the future of sight
the tablecloth in the wind
the open morning.

I am perfect, and make other things less so.
I am a vending machine; I replace all
those black men wearing white gloves.
I do not provide change.

I am the labouring furnace
the elevator door, half open
dreaming the passage of floors.
I do nothing for weeks
the urinals flushing applause.

I am the fuselage in the cornfield
the school bus skidding off a bridge.
Tick tock, my black box says
and I burn, consuming your
every breath, your last breath.

I am a reckless drive into the dark
where no tank lasts long enough
where no message can reach home
where none of this counts at all.

THEY ALWAYS SLIPS AWAY

A grass fire eats strawberries
a fruit packing hut
the outskirts of town.

A butt tossed out a speeding A-frame
maybe, or a weenie roast gone wrong
kids vanished, leaving only
their glowing sticks.
Flame smears the ditches
wrangles with wettish weeds
and, farther away, there's the sequined dress
of town, shaking its lanky goods.

The good ones sleep on
loving their pillows right back
while coins roll in the sky over town
with top hats and pill bottles and bones.
Happy little dream, frothy dream . . .

But here comes the dry broom.
Who knows why it happens?
Everything ready to go, and then
in a sinking minute, vapour.

The good ones jolt awake to see
a cloud on fire, raining stones
and the road out of town writhes
a snake held down
by a cruel, grinding boot.

Pick up our rapture at the travel agent's, pay with organs, patches of clear skin. You're not happy, fellow traveller, you mutter in bed, half awake, seeking a crumb under armpit. We collect string out there in the rain, with tourists and bus clang, and it's way too much to pay. What for? Just to sit around and complain? Books threaten me, they stand together in hallways shaking the maids down for cigarettes. I've got no sense of this as fun, grass headache and geyser of cheap coffee thrills. I need some chocolate, gunpowder, something to crack open my wooden eyecase. Loser, loser, the gluttons cheer, and I am kicked by the walls. Meanwhile, we are separated somehow in Sturgis, you in hot with bleach, me in a bag with the other pantyhose. Hey, says the river, get unified on TV. Roll up in the gutter for maximum efficiency. Frogs scream in ditch water and I walk a long dark road, what do you mean snakes? Still missing you and your enormous carnations. I want refried beans, you want refried beans, we all want refried beans. Coming across the Rio Grande upside down, waving our nice legs: Hello, brave new place I want to die in, hello! We can trade tools five times a day here, more vivid in our love affair than a car crash. We can sign the necessary forms, don the snowshoes, march-march into the city showers, praying for a real live resurrection. What we get instead is exactly what our parents got, nothing grand, just rotten little squirrels farting in the opera house. I'll have stopped doing something illegal by then and, relieved, pretend I'm exhausted, cards on the table, a chair tossed righteously into the hall. But for now, it's tourist time. There they are, the city fathers, yodelling under my fountain of dumb and weary hate. Me stumbling down alone, in the alone, with the alone, stuck on this fucking island, blessed to death.

WHITE HEAVEN

Joe Louis is not happy that dying men
call his name out in the gas chamber.
He is not standing on a cloud.

All over town the cabs ignore him.
Sandwiches are made for strangers.
Not for him, not for people like him.
Lovely women bend, bend in soft dresses
to kiss the feet of lesser men.

Joe Louis stands in a rooftop garden
staring a hole in the lacquered city,
watching the core begin to burn,
the festive straps of bridges come undone,
and cars, lighting the snowy avenues,
break down, fall open, empty themselves.
Joe is angry, Joe is black.
Money drifts down from heaven
and kisses him, kisses him
then wipes its lips.

WATER MAIN

Choking instructions arrive by train.
They wander the empty station
all night.
Mountain air rasping indoors
with its cargo of pine.

Embarkation lobby, lost and found
a tongueless fire bell hung near the ceiling
moaning and half charred
love notes dropped down the toilet's dry hole.

That's where it was found
down there
the swelled and purple water main
lurking in wormed mud
where murmuring animals and nettles
the contagion of stars
lullaby in the windless dark.

And here comes the cute how-to
reclining in sympathy on the tile floor;
shades of angel weeps on grave.

But see? the locked door down below
bulges in its damp bog
grateful for any listening ear.

YOU IMMEDIATELY BECOME DELINQUENT

I'm in a bank at night.
Snow falls on the wide wood floor.
Outside, gunslingers creep by
shaking their fists at me.
I am standing perfectly still
holding my breath
a blind cleaner to my left, listening.

An alarm goes off across the street
in the drugstore
its counter littered with pills
and children fall gasping
on the wide wood steps
their fat cheeks turning blue, white.

But I'm here in the bank
holding my breath.
The cleaner says:
You been here before
with that whirr in your chest.
He comes a little closer
breathes deep.
I know you, he says
and the bag of cash in my hand squirms
while outside, the children
float away on dry night wind.

THE WIFE YOU SAVE MAY BE YOUR OWN

Pay attention!
The telephone may be ringing.
Curtains blow out
then they blow in.
That is because the wind
comes through the glass
with its greasy tongue;
that is because the factories have blown up.
Pay attention!
The wife you save
accrues interest.
Little women in plastic bubbles.
Shake them up and watch it snow.
Lined up in a bank, clocks ticking
wind blowing, money dancing on TV.

The factory walls are gone
the factory floor still falling down
through stars and wind
down through the shaky molecules
of your house, your teeth and hair
through the shivering little girls
scuffing up snow in the vault
dreaming of the day you
wake up, wake up, wake up!

Tara Azzopardi

ALBANIA, 1925

We left Albania in 1925,
my mother packed a brooch, cocker spaniel
and a jar of pickled eggs.
My father shaved his body hair
and tied newspaper to his legs.
On the ocean, my father drank kerosene and perfume.
My mother gave birth to asthmatic twins,
they wheezed a concerto at night.
The journey lasted 52 days.
The twins nursed on the pickled eggs.
We landed in Montreal and worked in a laundromat 'til dusk.
We bought a shop for the brooch
and sold eyepatches for 12¢ apiece.
I grew taller than all and Albania became a memory,
a postcard,
an outdated part
in our modern-parted hair.

MEMO

At 2:33 p.m., we will stand
at the water cooler
and stare into nothing.

Resurrect and infect the imagination.
Cure conservatism with quinine and opium.
Infest the protoplasm. Teach hydrogen.
Embrace your doppelganger. Waltz the danse macabre.
Annihilate the upper class. Replace them with clairvoyant lobsters.
Congregate and sigh in séances.
Conjure the ghost of Lili Marlene. Elect her as mayor.
Spike the water supply with sonnets.
Rhyme in rhapsody.
Foresee futurists.
Pray for the plague of Joan of Arc.
Redefine hedonism in Glaswegian fashion.
Preach perversity. Repeat in sincerity.
Go out with a bang and be remembered.
Denounce apathy. Scream with the banshees.
Graduate the poet laureate to the poet inebriate.
Love with the intensity of a silent-film star.
Sleepwalk through the swamps.
Translate the song of swallows.
Regurgitate a saint. Begin again.

WITNESS OF THE PENNY ARCADE

I saw the straw break the camel's back
I heard the doves mourn their song
I saw the bibliographer of Bedlam
I saw the saints suffer from syphilis
I saw Victorians invent the Ouija board
I saw a couple neck in the neck of the woods
I saw Tom Dooley hang from a white oak tree
I saw the manatees sleep
I saw Lazarus drink the cup of hemlock
I saw a witch drowned in Salem
I saw the revolution, and the Fenians won
I saw Prometheus, Frankenstein and the Golem play checkers in a
        laundromat
I saw a Coney Island monkey living in a box
I saw Siamese twins sue each other
I saw a poodle attack a pitbull
I saw a honky-tonk jukebox spill the ghost of Hank Williams
I saw a pear embalmed in a jar
I saw Mata Hari smoke the hookah
I saw a Jacobean murder a Walmart
I saw a Berliner lose her eyelash, crying in a cabaret
I saw the punks pass out in the Chelsea Hotel
I saw the ocean dream a final undertow
I saw my bones in the soup pot
I saw the marrow go soft.

WHAT THE SHADOW KNOWS

Morocco is for the lonely and romantic.
The children love a Western star named Slappy Millshanks.
Monkeys know more than you think.
Japanese supermodels shoot ice from their eyes.
Psychics solve murders on the can.
Porgy didn't love Bess.
Russian boys make the best sailors.
Octopi cure hangovers upon request.
Gary Cooper talked to horses.
Orchids bloom on tears and milk.
The Revolution will begin with a Mexican named Lupe.
When you leave the room, the animals discuss you at length.

NEW ORLEANS, 1912

Mules chew sugar cane
Whipping their tails at cicadas and heat,
Tubercular prostitutes
Smoke hand-rolled cigarettes
Stewing okra with their feet.
Blues men gamble, forming bands.
Mermaids challenge beauty queens,
Cowboys tap-dance on tin
Mad Hattie shooting craps
With broken alligator teeth, and
Orphans are happiest here,
Drinking bourbon, drowning Mississippi time.

AT THE PARTY

There will be piñatas, shrimp with their tails,
Baked Alaskas, a cake in the shape of a cloud.

We will talk about Freud, pyramids
And the Green Lantern.

Phyllis Diller will tell dirty jokes
Vincent Price will teach French.

We'll play the Zombie game, strip poker
And True Detective in the bedroom.

We'll have a dog show, a dance-off
A beauty contest for Siamese twins.

A Swedish model will crawl on the floor, growling.

We'll dance to Joy Division and Neil Diamond
'Til three in the morning.

It will be the party
We'll never forget,
The party we'll never remember.

It'll be better than Roy Orbison, better than red velvet,
Better than Christmas in Tahiti.

THE ENEMY'S MOUSTACHE

The enemy's moustache is dark and foreboding,
We fear he trims it daily.
The enemy's moustache is cruel and unrelenting,
It harbours camels, sand and a time machine.
The enemy's moustache cannot be trusted,
Our leaders have mouths we can plainly see.
The enemy's moustache is a menacing black cloud,
It rains down upon us,
And interrupts our regular, scheduled t.v. programming.

BEDLAM, 9 A.M.

Waking wide, a haze of white
Bandaged ear to ear
Peter Lorre as the Doctor
Grinning, whispering
"Operation. Operation."

OCTOBER, 1939

Children wear Hallowe'en masks
Dogs tilt their heads, understanding

LOVE SONG

If we leave Sun Valley today,
Who will tend the goat-man's daughter?
Who will comb
Her wheat-grass hair?
Who will polish
Her nickel-gray hooves?
Who will feed
Her weevils and sugar?

If we leave Sun Valley today,
Who will keep the goat-man's daughter?
Who will tie her
To shade in summer?
Who will stroke
Her velvet-pink mouth?
Who will stand
To gently milk her?

THIS YEAR: REVOLUTION

This year Canada!
This year we take cold,
This year, revolution:
Humans on fours,
Animals in thongs
Sniffing crotches, wildly.

SUN-UP, SHOWDOWN

We sat in the saloon for hours
It could've been days
It could've been a dog's birthday
A sickly jury
A silver widow's anniversary.

Rain dripped from ceiling
To floor
We sat, silent
Inhaling sawdust, downing whiskey
Piano keys moving
Matilda laughing.

A rooster crowed
A donkey coughed
A rattlesnake slid from your boot.

We argued, bone-tired
Swearing each other
A Job's life through.

Lady's luck lasted all of nine months
And gambling men had had their day:
A fortune in gold, handkerchief tucked neat
A desert, a cemetery
Away.

Gary Barwin

SHOE

i am a trumpet, a black man, the first of july.

i was born on the back of the trembling earth without even a cradle, an iron, granite.

there were no trumpets but born without ceremony, they were not required.

i have divided myself in two, have studied violin. i shall follow the filigreed edges of my mother's dress as if it were a coastline.

we sail tomorrow, musclebound fishermen hauling their catch onto the boiling wharves.

i bought a saxophone, an anvil, some calipers.

we were sixty long days at sea, the nights were uncountable, unthinkable, corduroy.

on the twenty-second day, we bleached a sailor. we crossed the equator and i received a telephone call, a vision, a charitable donation. come down from the attic, it said, here's a hundred dollars.

the sun was holding the indy 500 on my back when i heard a knock on the door.

i never expected a brass band, a marmoset, tweed.

covered with leather, i tied a small knot, wore my heart on my sleeve.

yesterday, like bicycles, coin-collecting or rose-marie, i told the joke
about philately, but here i am, travelling like a ten-cent stamp on a
wide road that ends in malta.

we've all pitched in. hello, i said, but no one answered. i went up to the
podium but no one was there — not the orchestra, the manager, the
fifty-four kids all named joe.

perhaps it is time like a dolphin, the maji, an old suit brought back
from the cleaners.

i am a shoe, a radio, the perfect picture that didn't come out.

take me.

ARIA

there's a wolf on the roof
of my mouth
I'm ready to sing opera or
a small boat

a wolf in a captain's chair
navigating by moonlight or
the flaming hair of the maestro remembering potatoes

CHARLIE

if charlie my eldest brother had ever been born, he would have rolled in like fog.

no one would have been able to see me when he came in, just heard my voice calling from across the yard.

charlie, charlie, tell them to remember me, their other son, the one who covered the lawn with flour.

the roses, the patio, the grass all white. & when the wind blew, a cloud formed just above the ground, covered the windows, my hands, face, hair.

i was like a ghost or an angel, moving across the lawn. i called out to my parents, to my brother charlie. i made motions with my hands, let my feet leave the ground, arrived at the treehouse far above the cloud. from there i watched as the storm settled, as the yard returned to green.

charlie there on the swing set, my mother by the pickup truck. father was standing on the porch, his white mouth closed.

charlie, tell them that i am here waiting. i am pale but they can see me against the bedroom wall. look, this is where i am — you can see the curtain move as i walk by, hear the bed creak when i sit down.

BELONGING

I find an old brown suitcase in my bed.
I try to remember —
is the suitcase my lover
or grandma on another bender?
I don't think I'm married to it —
as far as I know my wife is out of town.
I approach the suitcase slowly,
you might say tenderly, for it is my belief that
over the last thousand years or so
we haven't been tender enough to luggage.

"Suitcase," I say. "Thanks for sharing my bed,
have you set the alarm?
Sorry, but I snore so loudly that
I've had to nail the blankets down
and I talk in my sleep —
things I wouldn't dare say while awake."

The suitcase winks its airline tags at me invitingly,
asks me to unzip it.
My hands tremble as the zipper moves around
its three dark sides,
the sound like a distant storm.
I open the suitcase.

An old man jumps out.
"Surprise!" he says.
"Uncle Henry!" I say.
"I've come to visit," he says.
"Uncle Henry!" I say.
He rips open his overcoat and a small deer jumps out.
"Meet my wife," he says.
Now I have a suitcase, Uncle Henry, and a deer in my bed.
Guess I'll be doing laundry soon.

"We travelled far," the deer says with a distant look in its eyes.
"We had no time to take our belongings with us.
It was cold.
The wind had many knives.
We gathered in groups and felt the sorrow Bambi felt
when he discovered animation."
"Sorry," Uncle Henry says with a shrug,
"we don't get out much.
But anyway, none of the family will talk to me
except you.
And funny thing,
here I am in your bedroom
and I feel like a nap."
Uncle Henry slides back into the suitcase and begins to snore.
The deer walks with me to the kitchen,
asks for a beer.

I have one too
and the deer opens them both with its small but impressive antlers.
"I never really fit in," the deer says.
"I never felt like I belonged
until I found that suitcase.
But it was many years before I discovered
your uncle Henry inside it.
I asked him, 'What were you doing in there all this time?'
'Trying to get out,' Henry said."

The deer shows me some photographs.
"We have children," it says.
"Beautiful brown velvet children with antlers like newborn teeth.
When we are together in our suitcase
Henry and I can hear the sound of the ocean in their tiny pink breaths.

For years we lived inside your uncle's overcoat.
It was all we had except for
the song our children sang

about a suitcase
left on a doorstep
by its lover.
The suitcase wept into the night.
Then when morning came
it promised itself it would be strong.
It climbed onto a luggage rack,
then into the cargo bay of an airplane bound for France.
The suitcase worked hard
never forgetting its promise
and one day it became President of England
and sang a song with the Rolling Stones.
It made a phone call to its lover
and said,
'I am the suitcase that you left on the doorstep
and now here I am Prime Minister of Spain.
Wait a minute while Julio Iglesias says a few words to you
and I ask the servants to buff my wheels.'
Oh it is a sad song," the deer says,
"but it fills me with gladness.

These long years, Henry and I have not rested but have travelled far
for I am a deer and the jobs are few.
But we have promised our children a life we never had.
The sun's warm curls creeping over the zippered edges of our suitcase,
the ocean's soft breath in our dreams,
the antlers of our children reaching upward
like branches finding bird's nests
waiting in midair."

"Deer," I say.
"You and Uncle Henry, the suitcase and all your children
have a place where you belong.
My bed is vast and the pillows are filled with feathers.
My wife, too, will welcome you
when she returns."

AFRICA

africa a planet splayed upon the earth, the milky way a knife-edge, glinting. here the moon is a spherical giraffe lost on the dark savannah, the thought of legs, neck, tail forgotten. the poem is an autograph, a masterpiece, a chevrolet that thinks itself a ford. we are driving towards nairobi, making an unearthly music in the glove compartment. we travel straight as a knife through a tiny planet, our long necks craned at the eclipsing moon. simon plays a tuba shaped like africa. i have always loved this coastline, he says, always loved this darkness, this poem, the milky way that fills our bath with stone. i am a zebra, the côte du rhone, the cylindrical name for bread. i hope you will not forget me when i remember my true shape. i am a masterpiece, a plate of spaghetti that has taken your name. i am an abattoir, a jungle, a dentist on the weekend. one day i will forgive you. now i remember your name.

I DON'T

have a face
walk on the green lawn
feel the absence of my face like a big pink ear

I arrive at the sprinkler

later
a limitless number of
mouth holes
cut in the big black sky

RECITATIVE

my brain is
my legs are
sixty miles down the road
someone finds
my single tongue
thrown (evidently)
out the window

PLANTING CONSENT

you were on the evening news

I carried the TV outside
buried it on a hill
with a beautiful view

by spring a small antenna
sprouted in that place

somewhere under the earth
clouds, blue sky and
the wingbeats of birds

WHATEVER-IT-WAS

a casket of weeping birds
the old kindness

last ship of the ancient dead
whiplash from a bell

the moon does not recall
whatever-it-was

the sleepy ground
called only the mind

pale blossom behind the eyelids

everywhere should whisper
in our footsteps

NOMAD

a dove returns
the wrinkled forehead
of its master
under its wing

Daniel f. Bradley

GO TO THE CORNER

count the next ten people to walk by
ten single people
wearing the same colour jacket
blue
count out ten blue jackets
and then wait
for the very next person
who has a plastic bag
follow them

LIVE LIFE LIKE IN A BEER COMMERCIAL

the light bounces around

above the city at the top

we crawl shadows

and a dark

light controls

the birds stay high

above and only shit

comes down

*

the waltz the bouncy bouncy i hate it when they sing the strangeness
of its tone cash n carry in french and the dry throat not
a day a foot in cold little feet the flash demand some
kinda bargain bouncy bunny ears patty cake smell
the capsule it's as simple as that it me don't you remember me
attached to are you new here never hear my name and home
owner the big strive to middle leather world i love
it when they sing this way the giant white twin set of trusting
paws fibre pink inside your walls the world gets smaller
and some days it gets very huge shirk or swim brown
eyes tear at my pink sweater illuminate siding iron of
seventy one my friends the school of rock kklc
the city of addiction not a threat if planes as bombs here spread
a little on me i'm into the care and washing of
your private parts i thought was new and interesting the
title was something seeks as attack in us tensions
it's all a bit johnny come slowly passing reference knows
a great deal about this dog gone it recovery from well
fair believe it rained in the desert last night the missing
twenty fourth missing the good sun moon we
have i have nothing under that sky hold tight
remember something while he was ripping stuff some
you don't know the headless statue of
lenin standing as a hostess of an
upscale mall eatery oh boy

*

stamped with mouseshrooming verse the vampire
of joy our newest sex toy welcome home twilight
of the goddess starting early this afternoon wishing
meat you in my pleasure a movie or a cup of tea
tell you of dreaming is to live on real
reel to reel is rarity we just walk on by walking
meat me at the turnstile filling up an idol
fade away radiate and watch the river flow
a road in gold just to have the cuffs of
jeans rolled up or knocked up or out knocked
the sadness that kinda lives in me go black to work
monday tuesday cut my hair bunny fucker's bag
in wool socks but who's the dog that needs to
ask forgiveness outside on a bench and
i slept for a whole bunch of hours unable to dream
out the lost days and days that i got here with
and to be so casual as to say what's going on
and not have to keep inside how i love the
details of my new spring jacket knew chew
is blue our revolutionary sweetheart remembering
goldberg equals al queda summer mystery
dance naked out line of the carpet of the
sun gold burns down who can take a letter beyond
the clouds who can take a nothing day and suddenly make it
a goddess always travels with her own shadow

UNIFORM MOTION DOWN A STAIRCASE

the home movies from
the prehistoric times before
colour projected the
dinosaurs moving slowly
fists scraping each other
the floor a puddle
of urine and a tea towel
covering your privates

for all
the dead cats
pushed from the top of the stairs
nose smudged into the dirt
of the corners smack
to the side of the head and
occasional blood all
over a carpet bends
into the pattern

this is history raised by the sky
and
flattened city
or at least made
the room very quiet
we could have all died
instead we get to bash
at each other

over by the museum
the lion backs into
its box

IMAGE AFTER LEAVES

the tongue slips
the last air
pissing out

sometimes we all make
sentences with meaning
defined and full
of content and the rest
is broken scrap
and wait
echo's weight

and it is as if
we carry all our
misspellings
in our chest
so full and heavy

to feel the
ground misstabs
armour
the snappy comebacks
and vicious circle

*

in the photo was held a stuffed animal where i had
a toy doll all cheaply printed this was a
credit card attached to thirty foot log that
i needed to carry through the restaurant that
housed a forest the bill was enough
to need a confirmation with all the recycling
of scripts that goes on it's easy to forget
this day started after the beheading that
there is no date just time breaking down the one
god universe to blame not sure that all the
length of the dead wood is needed sections
broke free as i dragged that card around
also i should explain the hallways stair
wells a clear glass protective barrier from
the public like one day woke up and
started stop making sense the detailed universe
with these feelings hitting my skin sister looking
so lovely and the kitchen light was real
so was meaning what we said she said
that's what's going on my father beginning this
conversation exactly the way he did three
minutes before exact words chosen the
ones we love without doubt the windows
and fall music to our here's nudge
and pleas kicking out too late to stop

GREEN RAY

*

we have extreme
banter the long sentences that
kinda fills the day being and
behaving both full time
*

night genteel
son touches
mother in a green light
across the waves
the last thing it did
before it went away
push the green away
*

a lake formed by two people
in the heights of human
interest in insects
begins in youth
wings legs
we don't sea
what hit us
*

in every single
language it means the same
trace it back to
the roots a hand
touches the head
animals in your own language
sun hides behind his
planet we end
other lives calling it food

*

through a life
direct killing of others
no single way is true
and anyone can
live longer than the
sadness in their heads
and any moment away
from the idea of that
memory
in a drunk's park
sharing a toke and
the words they make
us kill our children
*

mark of making
of something anything
labels you as strange
being
an object
that's not for everyone
i have no illusion my friends
my loves should have no interests
in mine we are
singles in doubles she walks
a head and makes our bread
i make our bed
sun our winter
tans move about
with no skill
*

fooled in happiness
ruled by the stomach
and
anyone is welcome
push the sand

*

because we know
the absolute sadness
beneath the fabric our
clothes cove the shape
and the soft dress flags
the eye away to
the corner
eye still see
eye still catch yours
eye filled with ache
anchors to each other
drift ((with evangeline, greg, john, bruno, then kim and ed dropped by
and words feeling skin with hairs attached kisses of living against death
we gulped words swallow the errol flynn's share all still word end in
silence as nods as silence meets me halfway and touch your head
breathe my beer for me just ask))
*

i know i'm in
when my pencil
is called venus
we decorate our
children with letters like they need names
somewhere to machines
people leave the message
where's the moon
*

our bodies are perfect
we are the only humans left a
porpoise fine wake
over the hips
slow ripples after the ankles
fine wake broken by the hand
travels in the light
the surface

*

what i can make
move the dirt
to another pile scrape the sides
jim gives me a sea sponge
bev gives me coral
i watch evangeline
float and still enjoy the way her
bottom floats a bit higher than her
shoulders
people know this
maybe
*

a photo for john barlow
these birds
swallow through the tunnel
live on pipe
above our heads
*

the city has everything
the waves race over
it all
up the coast
pitts
burgh toronto
*

or all the things that can happen
we're all oxygen
i'll take the next haul
one breath marks
your exhale
marks your period
the hours like days as sand
built into a square block
*

BLIND MASTERS

it all comes down to a matter of trust
and recent experiences
if you can't say anything
nice ass hole
don't say anything at
all always confused me
i don't know about your
ancestors but my
ancestors live in trees

Alice Burdick

OTTAWA IN SEPTEMBER

The unicorn on the wall
has a dry throat; is thirsty
and screams for a future.
Kingfisher fell into stone and now
can't leave the gate of power.

Cats meanwhile sit in the sun
and stare through the throng
of respectful visitors.
"I approve of this," she says,
"I really approve." And the squirrel leaps
onto the top of the partly melted bell.
Story of its pathetic ringing
carved onto a plaque.

Only can take a tour
to view glass flowers,
stained high and vivid.
Men walk the bridges over,
and occasional screaming reminds me
of the good old days.

Becoming popular is a trick
that can't fail. Falter through
the gothic arch, and step backward;
see houses of Parliament hover.
Stone space ships unable
to suck the humans up.

The sign in particular,
typeface of the country,
and the carved leaf,
strain in red plastic,
nailed to every building.

CIVIL SAC

Loving civility invites
no roses. The door is hinged
on the outside; it's easy to break down.

My face is full of shellfish
in semi-transparent wraps.
Chew belongings till they slide smoothly down
to previous worlds. My body is a rebel
to aspects of civility. It is an obvious history
of remedies and abandoned methods.

Treason to the holy word.
My body once held nutritious fluids,
the sacs and blood of possible being.

Lips on the tasty past;
sweet pop or soda
after small white pills.

BUTTER-MELTING TIME

Never mind the teething, distracted judge.
Very sad; hard vision's been blinded by the mirror.
One was declared dead, the next then to marry.
Not a nubile beginning,
crying at the family home.

These are the insured items:
braces for moose prevention; one fat-backed dog.

She is absent at her own funeral.
Bow on her chest is bigger than her head,
the better for hiding. On the couch,
hoping to be seen after so long.

Love to meet again.

The butter melts and it's appropriate.
Time to make time melt.
Wear one robe and leave the other empty on the couch.

What about molestation?
The originators in their island garden
never faced the obvious.

The acrobat spins above the graceful pool.

What will the clerk do at lunchtime?
Have visions in the office chair.

Glistening man emerges from water.
He's impulsive, munching carrots.
The carrots talk about companions,
flustered after the fall.

Another late afternoon of cross-dressing.
That hat looks good on no one.

No laughter in the annulling court.
The children know what's hidden.
Mother can't quite spit it out,
but she knows on whom the joke falls.

Father must find his way back into her bed.
Must be clever and ignore the broken springs.

MONSTER AIR

Monster drug ties his toes
and opens his big blues
to watch us crowd the hill.

The hill is so soft,
and ladies don't know what to say.
The air keeps my cat
on top of old knowledge.

Who needs the giant lady spider?
Half her body inside,
half her life gone.

GHASTLY PARCEL

Packed into the dull green truck,
a package will be delivered.
Ghastly parcel bought
by the privileged few
who won't view friends in sterile rooms.

Sharp light in dilated eyes.
Injured man is numb,
can only describe his harmed friends.

Orphan wants to see mother;
his handsome back is hurt.
He waits, broken, in the makeshift rest centre.

Bitter herbs, discrete bunch
dipped in salt.
An egg recalls birth, to eat.
Beauty is shielded from ugly truth.

HALIFAX DOWNTOWN, WINTER

The field for horses
shines with new ice.

They're not there,
holding up their limbs
and sweating under loose trees.

I CIRCUIT HOT FOOT

I circuit hot foot, blend into space camp. Carry the bridge over.
Eat a sorry apple. Sniff the rotting lake. It's full of life; I'll want it.
Barren body land accents glacial slide. Ice caps melt all the time.
World forgets own rules.

Seagulls are mad for wood posts. Can't stop loon song and wouldn't want to.
The work of interrogation is just begun. Change the swinging
light bulb. Seen as a Jewish girl before I knew. Declamations not enjoyed.
Capital city wants new coin.

Not a sex conference, not that kind of workshop. Phones hear one side.
Cords lengthen into the void. Breath short. Work on length. Air
burned by cigarettes. Something in the way we breathe pleases lovers.
Exhalation breeds hunger. Eggs are placed in a plastic bag, swung and
released. Devoured.

Constant hummingbird in dead birch tree. Oddly loud and bursting
sounds. Fragrant wild flowers. Bubblegum melts in foil and chews funny.
A fireball is a boat. Sanded then to travel. Memory gladly tells
statues in Belgium to recall the original peeing boy. Troughs of water spray.
Really good beer.

Small delicate hunters. Abandoned baby bird stands tall, searches sky.
Shirtless landlord prefers not to be heard cussing. Nipple ring glints
from gray froth of chest. Authorities gravely intone place.
Space crumblers. Heart holders. Dissolving salt in palm of hand.
Clockwise dogs. Fire-loving deer. Smokey the Bear starts fires, secretly.

Smoking love letters brand tall trees. Stroke friendship, cup love, lap desire.
What lines bind these? Why do rules vary? Breasts drip sweat from crease.

Flagpole bears no flag. Happy accident. Humour varies subtle bodies.
Sit cooking sun. Cricket party. Visible lifeline. Tea bag sits sadly elevated

in high flat sink. Mention of phallic mushroom invites no response.
Its brew suits a drugged god. Urine sanctifies bad ideas.
Incidental bird box.

Greatness abounds in small rooms. Silence incorporates desire and the
passing of time. Best left alone. Good music flavours my mouth.
Additional room holds dry and live spiders. Unseen webs, but solid bodies
drop apparent.

Logic says a step onto a low deck means wet feet. No empty man.
Body makes strange sounds all the time. Matter of stomach to be faced.
Brilliant yellow earwax. Tanned woman bares teeth through bright pink
lipstick. Not to be disturbed. When she says, "Here comes the big bear,"
a small tan dog runs up.

This water is very green. When you look down through its surface, you
can see the bottom rise. Sea absorbed by growing mud. Moss and algae
hold the gathering chain, pull it lower, make it green.

Children's books line shelves. Adults write books for children.
Psychic asks leading questions. My feet get dirty very fast.
That's just the way it is: world of dust. Little boys veer out into traffic.
Gain speed so bikes may leap piled mounds.

Haven't seen a stork in a long time. I miss storks. Hear the occasional
loon bawl. From shallow mud, pincers point up. What separates bird from
man whistle? Melody. Truck rumbles past. Air moves, light full of clouds.
Soft brown sofa. Can't always explain why one desires another.
Mortification of strange comments. Told not to wonder what is real.
Will skin soon be tasted?

Butter takes precedence. Touch discovery of bruises on thighs. Wrestling
moves onto floor. Under sheets, darkened lights, pattern of leaves on wall
at night. Polaroids dictate new faces. Beans take on garlic and lose. Heart
wrapped in skin of dragonfruit.

Taste delivers memory. Moistness of skin on skin. Lake People is open for
floating. Body waves break sweat. Already well known by strangers.
Technology grits teeth in its phantom grace. Broken farce of bits that prevail.

Taste in music slightly off. Long lashes, laughs of excitement.
Slide down me. I'll feel your scars thus. Men with low waists
are not like you. They titter next to chip trucks under the hot sun.
Your broad chest, broad hands, are spread thick with flesh.

Pass muster as a pretend patient. Suffer the ways to fail.
All I know is the hold of things learned. Heart asks, Huh?
Answer heart, Listen. Litmus of known words. I've heard
doubt that words invite hope. Words bring hope! Heart feels words
and translates through fingers and brain. Organs slide, hard to hold.

My buttocks invite trouble. Fingers and toes match lengths.
Cakes made of lard melt fast. Owners constantly encroach on land.
Discomfort in wait, the wonder to scram. What of the need to shower?
Paid visitors make this uncertain.

Pill dares not disturb headache, writhing under brow bone. Teeth every
which way. Wonder if visible, they'd tear muscle. View of skeletal system.
Through which glides a rosy map of rivers in all directions.

Surge of blood. Pulse of air. The distance is great.
Various mints climb sunshine. Thin the air clean.

Slippery funk in backyards. A new hoop to pull the light down.
Advent of technology nears no horizon. Is there rain?
Blind flash of lightning. Neck bent out of window.

Musculature holds stream of body. Firm up after runs.
Air in the morning steams hops and yeast. Ill cars fart exhaust.
Older men like my shape. Realm of nostalgic attraction.
It's not necessary to drink coffee.

Declared division between architects and hockey players. Of these teams, I own no parcel, and yet cheer on. Some wheels speed up as I cross streets. Women stand early in orange uniforms of labour. Work to hold signs. Thin mirror of stress. Static sense that work hovers between fluorescent glare and cool tiled floor.

No clearance to move. To be moved is a human state.
Be a man. Be a woman. Be aware that the borrowed cat lies with his head in a bowl of water. His world upside down. Context is malleable.
I wish I had a heart that folded out into sharp waves of air and electricity. Meanwhile, to be a conductor.

Define earthquakes as rumble of blood through fleshy corridors.
Boat tacks. Nautical terms slide down smooth sides into standard lexicon. Some knot holds fast the listing boat before she slithers off into the waves of the middle channel.

Baffled talk of coelacanths and mammals. Who asked is a bird a mammal? Long paths are older than large houses. Lupine grows tall to tell its scent further. Its colours show a striping love of blue sky, green leaf. Always a man stands, scythe in hand to cut the earth down. Constant betrayal of growth not a lesson learned. Perpetual blade to life. Habit helps no plant.

Happiness is not something to muster. It's given and then sent on. Harsh method. Long wait just to find we belong to humanity. Notions stick to the interior of the skull, moist current of skin. Nice that items are offered, but can one accept into one's possession another's thoughts? Can one give to another something not available to be owned? Inevitable errors show how much time forgets.

Moist grass in large park. Sticky dark air wants to glide.
Sweat is incorrigible. It cooks bumps in private places.
They swell and it's embarrassing. People keep eyes open to their own invisible ways. Dramatic annoyer seems to hate rhubarb.
Doesn't see the purpose!

Clothes wave wanly on the lowering line. Twine rolls across the floor,
at no great speed. Wavering attraction rides a big boat.
Sailors grow muscles through spinach. Legumes gather force in the fridge.
Sign: Complete Auto Ser

Worry meanders casual through the veils of day. Parts trucks and peers
into crevice called heart (sometimes mind). Down in the hollow,
petals moult onto turquoise fields. A long time to traverse the wide valley.
No longer a simple matter of pointing, then gliding into the void.

Now eyes glisten from memory and wind and dust swirled up by boys
on fast bikes. They are wise, and donned thin white masks in advance.
Therefore, they had no unexamined tears. Bite a lip and hop a mound of
possibly toxic earth.

Soldiers in full green and mottle stand at the back door of an empty
store. Look up as I pass. Red rim to blue eyes, hopeful that the hopeless
trial shall soon end. All closed doors shall eventually open. Stale time shall
go. Corners of dust shall release old secrets into tunnel of sunshine.
Large murderous buildings shall tilt and bend and lighten up.
Why did we take it all so seriously?

TROPHIES

The daughter of the tricky one
knows she's in the shadow of the living room.
She calls down the donkeys who know their paths,
the strong pull
of small children.

Shuttled steel strings.
Large soap bubbles
want to burst.
Glamorous metal bees.
Man wants what the dog ate.

The life room is lined with trophies,
or what one wants to call garbage cans.
Somehow a city beyond the trees.
I've been framed.
Ask the preacher why he hates me.

Luckily there are the famous:
I'm an official named General Disturbance.
The coast is out.

Some can never really die.
They crouch from the dead to the bed.

LUNCH PAILS

Old times.
Twelve lunch pails.
Twelve men's dress shirts
to wash and iron,
and remember the one
who didn't come home.

Making sandwiches,
the widow holds her baby mind.
She can die and see a wreath
before that time.

Being touched and spiky.
The hard memory
of never seeing a father.

The candid talk of a day,
bombed, and the soldiers around
the bedroom walls.

Home,
and a belly full.

Kevin Connolly

REPOSSESSION

When they board up the hobby shop
only the moon notices — and the stationary
conductor waving in a train no longer
circling the village, but caught forever
in a chilly tunnel two peaks
north of the cheerless alpine church.

Down front, lead children
mock-shiver in the town square,
their little schnauzers parked mid-bark,
the painted hands pawing for
the rigid mothers, painted sisters,
gathering wool beside the Candy Shoppe.

Behind City Hall, past tumbleweed
flosses of silica snow, little train-model
glaziers slap train-model putty on train-
model trowels next to the lifelike factory,
where tradesmen stir simulated liquid
in a building without interior walls.

Out there in the genuine moonlight,
trees are still trees, light remains light,
but the die-cast freeway ducks the question,
closes up shop, turns its armchair
toward the audience and bellows out
the sorry business of the world.

DRIFT

The Killim Haus, Delia's Esthetics,
Shwarma Hut, all of them duck before
the same sullen pleasures —
the village of tomorrow undone
almost by accident, a loose coalition
of strip malls and strip malls and strip
malls: Quik-E Convenience,
Cheers Fine Foods, Fish and Cheeps:
a pet store. In the absence of real stars
repetition has its consolations —
random lights conscripted into the opera,
reconfigured as sheet-metal thunder,
Sea of Rains Dry-Kleen,
two-for-one Szechwan lobster.

What endures, a piece of it, is weather,
the snap and cuddle of clouds,
on-and-off pressure of traffic,
treasured debris of childhood
cohabiting the same shrunken rooms,
the same lint-frosted air ducts,
the same breezeway assignations after
bridge or curling or cribbage:
Where's Dad? Did Beth leave?
Who signed what in who's yearbook,
who conjured the calamity — the deep
tension-emptying sigh before
the garage door dumps its
overload of impossible light.

It's all good because it's all decided.
The dream mall is closed for business,
its flummoxed architect returned
to Europe with his tale between his teeth.
But who'll hike out the salvage?
The anchor-stores crumbling, time-
shares stuttering, the buckling credit
of the jury truants: *No flyers, please;*
No one home; Not at this address;
all of it a tough-love lesson in
the pitfalls of earnest simulation.
Desperation among the toothpicks:
unlit gatehouses, empty parking
booths, hard edge trembling in a
wilderness of signs.

WINSLOW HOMER

after Pete Winslow

1
to wander a cacophony with the north wind as stoolpigeon
is to draw silence from a well kick it in the scrotum then
pronounce it unfit to drive

2
to scale Everest towing a Zellers baby stroller
is to strand the sun permanently in a socket
tedious to the elderly

3
to erect a courthouse of baseballs and forcemeats
is to coax democracy toward its final euphony
the flies all shagging the dogs

CONTRACTUAL OBLIGATION

salucle. Good afternoon. I'm a little baby. *in fan tulus*
I know I don't look like a little baby, *infantis specie*
but I can assure you that I am. *id firmum et actio habet*
I thank you all for coming this evening.
I'd also like to thank this afternoon's sponsors:
the sun, walnuts, Parma ham,
and the Woody Permanence of Chairs.
And I'm sure you'll join me
in expressing your sincere gratitude for
bending, stretching and branding,
for rain, wind and rectitude.

I'd like to thank you all for coming
on this windy evening, full of promise;
I thank you not merely
on behalf of myself, a little ham,
but on behalf of our guests — sun,
wind and the woody rectitude
of permanent rain. I'm grateful for
your gratitude, for your bending
and your wilting, and especially for
your support of our major sponsor,
Sunny Walnuts.

I'd like to thank you all for coming,
but remind you to clean up after yourselves.
Did I mention the little baby?
That I have the great good fortune of being
he on this rainy, woody afternoon?
Of course, quite right, I mentioned that
in closing, before we welcomed
our guests, but after we thanked our
sponsors: wind, rain and branding.

Thanks for coming, really,
if you'd all just shut up and take your
seats, our breathless evening of thanks
and sincere gratitude can finally begin.
And now, ladies and gentlemen, I'd like to
turn your attention to the woody clearing
at the opposite edge of the stage.
On any other windy evening, it is Rectitude that
would be sitting there, but of course,
on grounds I'm sure are repugnant to you
and I, both as loyal babies and as little hams
in our own right, Rectitude is playing
rock hockey in a foreign country none of us
could pronounce correctly if we tried,
so let's stop trying, shall we?

Good morning. I'm a little baby.
I'd like to thank our sponsors,
who I believe you now know personally,
and I'd especially like to thank you all
for coming on this windy evening.
Thank you all. If you'd please, please,
please, just take your seats in the
clearing, we're ready to begin.

HOOKS

after Darrell Gray

The hooks of panic and obliging bloodhounds.
The hooks of winter, torched ragged trees.
The hooks in the mirror, cramped, dumbstruck.
Amorous hooks, scuffling on escalators.

The hooks of kinship, the hooks of promise.
Solitary hooks hung in crooked doorframes.
The hooks that stir and shimmy down the drainpipes.
The hooks of wonder and of doubt.

Meat hooks.
Paper hooks.
The hooks of obsolete species.
Hooks perched on a moment's peace.

The hooks of night birds, plotting against daybreak.
The hooks that groan in everything you touch.

DEPOSITION

Wreath of shadows
breathless in the doctored
darkness, take my testimony,
conjure carjacks in a junkyard,
clothe the runways in a
cave of white.

Cowl of doorframes
lifeless in the noon sun,
drop your dark suit carefully,
walk the gravel to the causeway,
whisper vengeance to the
shards of evening.

ARCHITECT

I imagine a corner as
four corners, on which
sit four traffic lights and four
blocks, soaring into four cubes,
four towers, overlooking
countless over-lit squares.

Thus is a life brought to ruin —
street by dreaming street.

IN LIMBO

wild hares crawl up the ass of no one,
so breathe easy
in the cluttered vestibule

There's time,
the day implies, hopefully perhaps:
hot bright rusted grass

Time revels in its gaunt celebrity —
all tilt and counterpoint,
a drowsy feather hovering in a maelstrom

Like thunder dwarfing a stickpin,
or just a dogfly dodging water boulders
over a swollen culvert, the brave

beetle highboards sawgrass into
swinging air — life is heavy, breath
the trauma of butterflies

DETAINEE

I was questioned for bartering with beggars
I was arrested for squandering winter silence
I was accused of fleecing skittish sheep
I was detained for breaking wind successfully

I was questioned on a sudden turn of weather
I was arrested by an ant, mighty for its size
I was accused of exaggerating a sunrise
I was detained for fingering the moon

I was questioned for cutting a river's current
I was arrested for slackening a man's memory
I was accused of shimmering without a permit
I was detained for stains on my conscience

FINGER LAKE

There is a lake
in the scene above my body
that no one dares to touch:
a question, a rumour
clothed in throaty silence.

From where I sit,
drowning in the garden,
I watch my fingers
fishhooked by its
briar of stars.

PIANO GAG

the grapes of wrath decant
the leaves of grass devein
the wines of spring declaim
the branch of yew debarks

every malice has its window
every kraken has its wake
every tipster has his scoundrel
every dullard takes his cake

is it a matter of redress
that makes me so digress?
does a thunder torn asunder send
me blundering toward the sauna?

gag the piano and bait the snare
love is cruel and life, unfair

INDULGENCES

We stood there panting, gathering ourselves for action,
while the plummets optioned, and Gus the Birthday Clown
alienated everyone with the chain-smoking and those dog-shaped
balloons. Dust gathered under the Instacopy, the no-account
counter help picked pimento from the chicken loaf while
we stood there panting, gathering ourselves for action.

Years pass and we're poised to clone Christ.
Just to be certain, we take scrapings from a dozen of the
oldest souvenirs. Within months all samples reveal
a tiny replica of one Alfred Wolfram of Dauphin, Man.
"It's our mistakes that define us," he'll say later in scores
of televised addresses. "We adore them, to be totally honest."

And so we dawdle, knocking tines from a chandelier of sorrows.
Dirt and ugliness await me in the places we know.

William A. Davison

At night I am visited by beings who eat human hair.

A FLY FOR A DOCTOR

This stinging
And the disease it occupies
Under my chin
I fly tomorrow
For a doctor
Or a dog of volcanic ash
That leaps upon me
Sexually
And tips over the balustrade
Glasses of urine
I doubt they are witness
To more problematic ventures
Than the microscopic odyssey
Of twenty flaming turds
On a raft between rivers.

YESTERDAY I THINK

The helping hand launch pad lift office grab baggage stop go backwards Neoist lunch shit package go to the weird railway station and be inverted over truck cap laughpad you can't tell me to go pull the wool over your eyes said backwards man to the Penelope calliope organ grinder finder weather veins bulging in gray sky demons eyes in the back of my truck I said to the mother assistant that very day she wore her blue nylon windmaker and it windy it really windy too you said I could look for brass hooks real tarnish varnished bananas cabanas for tune fortune in the room of gloom boom he goes crack back to the black sack for the clap trap rat carcass rotting in my teeth crack snacks for big mutant bastards hullabaloo glue.

I went to the store and bought fifty helpings of sandwitch hats to take to the old folks back home at the north poles why would I waste my time here in this old sand doom when I could be eating pie in the back room of her fabulous saloon but no I wait in this cloudy costume all day long all week month year after year just to find she's gone back to the station with this fucking cockroach guy I can't believe I could be so stupid to think that she hadn't any idea where to go that night but there she went that away she said pointing up her skirt while the fucking rain poured down on us like black sheets in the wind.

This has got to be here somewhere over death over dressed up to go nowhere but to live in evil black soup or on evil black soup whichever is the first to come spilling into the room on the canned cancer ward floor bore ing me to dead moments of tears in the cloth of my eyes the blue spots won't come out to play in the rain because of all this rain I said to her but then it stopped raining for once and everyone smiled and I licked the back of her hand and got stuck on the ring of truth.

It all wasn't alright I knew it would be hard but this isn't getting any easier to swallow flew into the ward and around and around the poor patient with the head wound bandages unravelled like tired old stories told once too often or like my not so favourite pass time in a bottle of old 44 guzzled down gullets of gold or pinched behind hospital curtains going down going down down into an abyss of sexual melancholy hurting glances in the shadows of her smile but too tired to resist I drank poison walkers walked out of the ward with know glasses on and keeled over in the ambulance bay which was polluted with dead fish drinking smells of exhaust fuming over baggage left to dry in the sun pools of light spilling over my wounded corporal.

Then it hit the bottom of the tank and I sank along with it lifted not by my spirits which were soggy and damp like my boots which were not of rubber but of some kind of fish scales of justice tipped tipsy drunken boat in the laneway in the way of some truck making deliveries of liver he's waiting inside for his liver to come so he can fall asleep with all his organs stapled to a piece of cardboard on which he had drawn a stick figure representation of himself as he had been before the accidental figure crashed through his living room on a broom.

It couldn't have happened yesterday but it did I think.

THE LIONS OF MEMORY

The great husks of our lives lie in wait.

Beneath the bellies, the lions of memory, sour and foul, caress the waiting, terrible stillness.

THE BREATHING MATCH

I've had a spill. I took a tumble. I've fallen into a useless torpor of a divine breathing match with an indignant bear on the one side and a length of string on the other.

A NIGHT SPENT WITH SEVERAL SPECIES OF BIRDS

I rinsed my blood with an acid bath when the phone rang. It was an unearthly crow. Calling about all the noise last night. I hid under the sheets with a pickle clasped tightly in my hand. I could tell it was a smashing invention although when Virginia popped out of the cupboard all nude and shiny like something I'd half forgotten, I licked the back of my hand and it tasted of gasoline. Where are the wheels for this damned thing, I can't go very far like this. The heart was still pumping on the sidewalk, I could not walk away. I saw a condor drifting through the office building with a gold chain hanging from its mouth. It was inscribed with a secret diagram resembling genitals. It flew without flapping and was accompanied by white noise. I raised my gun but was swallowed by the avalanche.

THE ACCIDENTAL NUMBER

I tasted the soup of victory under the weathered boards of the veranda and a raccoon was there in the semi-darkness and was whistling something vaguely familiar and I could hear my mother walking about above me but her shoes were not of this earth but were a kind of shadow material that made her footsteps seem out of time.

The taste was bitter and made my tongue shrivel like a dried-up old leaf blowing around under the veranda and my father's car came into view through the slats and it sounded like thunder and the accidental number was painted on the door and he stepped out and he was just a silhouette of a starry night and the dog ran so fast its fur caught fire and I burst through the boards with a bucket of water.

ACCIDENTAL ORGASM IN A CARDBOARD BOX

I down against that old mill and suddenly water is there in two-feet-thick asparagus. It tickles this foot pedal cranking out tunes of rusty Penelope. The grave is waiting in an envelope, black hearts often follow me. But only the music of particular angles is captured in this lens.

The outside. The force, the manipulation of sound and rubber. The glandered secretions and coughing fits. This is what we've left behind in that decaying bag.

I gripped my plastic fork with a religious intensity. It squeaked and shrank away and now the sun is in the room all drunken swagger and furious fists. A pounding cock leapt up from behind the cardboard architecture and the architect dropped his scissors and ran for the skirts. The surf is silent, sucking oranges.

Miasma threw her cylindrical hat against the carapace. It cracked open and the crab inside was not a crab but a blood spirit. And it took out its teeth and flung them against us. And we collapsed into the sand and were lost.

It was no accident our penetration of the darkness. It came after belief was crushed and lingered in the moment of hopelessness. It was no accident at all that our bicycles were made of bread as hard as steel and we fell into the speed of dreams.

A chamber pot overturned in the road. We swerved to avoid it but our gears became all rubberish and no longer served us. A turd crashed against the grille. The vehicle crumpled. The momentum was insufficient to kill us so we got out and bashed our skulls in with a hammer. I cannot say why.

This is where the cardboard box comes in. You see, we were gathered up by some vagabond and our corpses placed inside it. There were other corpses in there, some of animals, some... unknown. It was strangely soothing, we could hear him whistling. A gentle light poured through the folded flaps. Our disintegration was much quicker than I would have expected. We joined the mass of bones and fur and became a new creature and for a time we were happy. Then we were dust.

ROLLED A DOZEN YEARS BACKWARD

The sick eyes of the train conductor slid sideways over his newspaper. We caught a glance reflected in the blood pool but our candied dresses caught fire like sandpaper kisses and languid ghosts rolled over in the blistered nightmare of my bed. The conductor sucked on the licorice dog tail as we rolled our barrel of flame past the tar pond where pubescent children dissolved in a knowing embrace.

THE ANT SONG

Tree buzzer no work. It gone all dead. This morning when the rain came and my pants split lip to reveal elastic thunderwear. Lifting the dead wood hands from the riverbed I sing the mother melody. I sing the ant song sing while lifting dead wood hands. Mother collapse all over the mountains. Where is her hand? Where thunder claps and sings the song of hands clapping. The wet hands fly from the water. The ants in pants split the scene seam seen leaving in large motorized numbers.

I came upon seven numbers of fallen wood trees drifting in the dried-up riverbed. Licked the ants with flicking tongue. Split open tree trunks to reveal plastic ants dancing. The season of the wooden carcass is hot. Smells drift up from the riverbed.

This is today's delivery all covered with chocolate and it bursts through our hearts like a blade of solid grass. This is yesterday's turd drying in the sun, it rains only under my umbrella and all the cats whisper about me in their secret language. This is tomorrow and tomorrow and tomorrow and it's not here where I left it but it couldn't have gone far on gangrenous legs you know. I limp towards the decision with the green-faced doll all glowing sexually. I mathematically converted the silent portions of love into water (or blood into dogs). Where are the answers now? Where are the questions?

Elena sat down on the pedestal with a handful of pubic hair. She tightened her collar just a little for the appropriate shade of blue. I stroked an alligator handbag instead of language. She knew my intentions were plastic and decoded all the messages with twirling fingers.

"Elena," I whispered. "You have caught an eagle in your hair."

I was lying of course.

"I know you're lying." She lifted her gaze from the spot on the tiles and smiled feverishly.

"Returning tomorrow is never good enough. It slips under the door like a carpenter's fish." I returned her smile with several twitching follicles.

Her grip slowly loosened and I could see that the tiny hairs had undergone a strange metamorphosis. It was difficult to say just what they had become. A stork? A steam engine? A drop of semen? It was somehow compelling.

"Where are you taking me?" she sputtered through the cloth.

We were in a car, moving through a bleak and desolate landscape. It was twilight. The countryside had been blown apart under heavy shelling. Faint shadows moved in the craters.

"To the carnival," I replied.

I was lying again. A moment passed in which all the apes in Africa screamed at the heavens. I hurled myself from the moving vehicle.

It comes as no surprise to learn that you can't rely on the mysteries of life to fall neatly into place like a tangled row of seaweed or five hundred accidents of nasturtiums or wasps wrapped in carbon paper. You have to believe in the sunshine, in the strength in a lion's jaw, in the propitious nature of magnetized nails.

"You have to believe. You have to believe. You have to believe."

The voice from the plastic box kept repeating.

HOSPITAL NEVER REMEMBERED

I fill my head with water until my brain is now floating
It is painful but necessary
Then it comes
A tiny boat across my head ocean
A light it is faint but sufficient for navigation
Now I am crying again and the fabric is tight across my forehead
The skin is black and the swelling now noticed by my wife
The wounded are arriving as my fingers falling to the floor

THE EGG IN MOUSTACHE TROUSERS

The reverberant spring swung down from the heavens on several silver hairs. It caught the light in coils like a snake might do if cornered by an incessant reflection. We prepared for the boiled egg arrival by walking on pennies and lifting our legs over our heads with every cautious step. More carcass than pillow, Walter shovelled the steam into the furnace bag with a quick flip of the flipper finger. Egg, egg in moustache trousers came rolling down the hill in back of the old house, a galloping horse close behind. It was raining but not in the usual way. It was cat fur that fell from the sky that day, all shiny and black and the sun went wandering. The egg in moustache trousers received a package from Walter Thumbgardener. Inside the package, a deadly, tiny, coughing pellet of sarcastic wit wrapped in the skin of the flea collector. Walter was living in the package with a number of shrinking relatives. At last, the egg approached the package with glimmering shears. The old house was alive with the rolling sun as fur settled on every surface. Snip! The strings came unglued one by one. A brittle pocket of mesmerized ocelots began singing.

In the distant ocean, a face began to boil.

HATS!

Hats! How they stream by in the thousands. Alive with the knowledge of their emptiness and their colours glowing through teary eyes. I envy their persistent happenstance. But they moulder in an instant! They are not happy! How can they be when their boats have sailed without them! I ask you, is this any way to treat a lady? A lady with iron teeth and a long, tall, cylindrical body with tiny wheels at the bottom and a HAT with flames for feathers and a horse's head for a handbag! Then again, it makes little difference. They will laugh at anything! They know all the answers. They make up the answers as they go along!

The stream is carrying them away from me now. I feel much calmer, alone and dead behind my newspaper. Thank you for the lovely carnival.

UNTITLED OCCURRENCE

High in the palms, a small, gray light slowly entered a coconut.

Beatriz Hausner

DOWN

Gather your parts in the morning:
they have been served and lie at your feet
as you get off the bed and realize
that the room is full of claws and shadows
growing gray under your feet: above
the sky is slate and cold air. Inside
the furniture moves with the wind howling
in the corners of winter which grows roots
in the foundations of the house.

No one is behind you yet they follow
his shadow prolonging your darkness
as you enter the rigidity of the clock
where the lines are straight driving
the fury which fills the ancestral bundles.

Somewhere deep inside shards of laughter
pierce the darkness. Your ghosts clamour to get out
leave the sealed boxes invent a new phoenix of flesh
and blood enter the sun.

GHOST

In my dead friend's dream
I too dream a dream where
I am to eat fifteen percent
of the soup left uneaten
by his dog's ghost.

My ghost is a living cat.
He hangs from the lamps
stands on his head curls
into furnishings that mirror
the lives of domestic animals
wanderers inside prairie mind
guarded by my ghostly selves.

MOTHER OF SOUND

Mother of the ideal man
begins her daily climb
up the stairs of heaven
large muscle inside writhing
pushing out through her mouth
entirely of sex the infinity
of swelling children lifting
the sequins off her dress
red feathers fluttering between
her hands mother of sound
rhythms rising from Aretha
woman colossus her
fingernails are piano keys
music for her son in my arms

MY NEW BAG

Brown outside silky
brown inside the new
bag came in the mail
neatly folded I opened its
edges and discovered my
dependents had installed
their landscapes of water
and earthen surfaces gifts
for a heart fed by arctic rivers.

Now that it's spring swallows
fly in and out of the bag of
forest leaves. I enter and begin
my daily walk down its zippers
into a pocket which opens into
prairies where chiefs
who threaten to poison
the contents of my bag
live in chains.

Many legs burst out of my bag
as we rush down the street
emptying our fires and our pleasure.
Formerly stored in its corners my
selves delve deeper into the bag
where the little people are delicate
despite their habit-acquired love
of living with big cats inside
my brand new bag.

JE NE MANGE PAS DE CE PAIN LÀ

I once worked for a cruel woman.
Angry and tired she grew hoarse
in her silence while we shouted
our complaint to the tutelary
gods of the workplace weaving
our tears into elaborate garments.

New demonic Alice, her elastic neck
hung over us as she served the bitter
meal of twisted shrunken limbs. She
excelled at preparing elaborate dishes
whose assembly she followed obediently
from a book of rules inscribed
by invisible fat superiors whose metal claws
she dutifully polished until they glowed.

Time has passed. Today, I sometimes see
her eyes gazing at me from the soup
I carefully stir in my worst nightmares.

LAWRENCE WEISBERG SWALLOWING HIS TONGUE

When he met us at the square
smoke rose from his shoes floated
in the air like a song suspended
he treaded the beaded lining of
the ground. He claimed he came alone

though we knew that he walked alongside
the nurse from outer space visible only
when he opened his immense chest of
treasures. He carried fire inside him burning
deep and wound tightly like a fist pounding
at the growing silence of this age.

He pulled his tongue inward stretching
the limits of endurance suffering the song
as it imploded with his heart.

                         Here was a
lion whose pelt was lined with sun bird
feathers big cat accustomed to hanging
from lamps in the first house where he
lived with his sister priestess of the dance
and magic animals that shine in the night.

STREETCAR MADNESS

> *"La beauté sera convulsive ou elle ne sera pas"*
> — André Breton

I ate my kitty's paws. The tail too.
On a streetcar I devoured him
bite by bite front to back stalled
traffic whizzing by we sat

beating our hearts into
edible heat. At the lights
we reclined the seats sighed
rolled towards a humid

station climbed the backbone
of madness spied an enormous eye
grew elegant lips. Our knees met
at the top of the escalator.

The merry citizens lived out
their secrets inside the briefcase fruit
moaned fish longed for the ocean
cool pleasure water filled

the change box. My kitty licked
his whiskers and settled on the armrest.
Instantly the driver's raw voice
turned on my windows jealousy

filled the air teeth rattled
softly sinking into vinyl
seats your carnivores made
the lady passenger in me

blush. Words expired
caught in the jaws.
At the next stop we switched
to the express lanes raced
towards the authority of the clock
which died when we rang the bell
our baggage began to bloom.
Hide, cat. When your goodness

exits strange eyes will fill
the distance between your fingertips
and my tongue. Other ghosts will sit
next to me wearing

sunflower masks one thousand
eyes will search out the closed landscape.
Invisible inside your briefcase
I eat the libidinous apple.

My unessential pasts are put
to rest and soon the streetcar comes to
a halt. Inflections pronounce your stripes.
Let's play hide and seek and I will find

you upside down in the corner
and with my nails wear down your
linings. Locomotion is maddening.
Artificial jungles grow inside

the rearview mirror. Seated standing
the travellers sweat ink.
Where is the true cat? I sense your
breathing approaching bearing

gifts the wireless letter grows
roots back in my garden.
Let's climb on the roof.
Once the others wilt we'll hang

from a glance and watch your skylights
while the woman inside
uncovers a basket overflowing
with eyes for you for me.

RIDER

He comes. The sky is near
his new self abandons
the strange animals he inherited.

He rides a horse made of gold
wears his heart invisibly
stitched to mine and enters the room.

The eye of the storm watches
from the window: I have
his tongue caught in my mouth.

JUST MAN

Ideal man never fails to turn himself
inside out for love of the dispossessed.
He eats bitter meals made of their
detached eyes. Quivering he listens:

the murmur of their pain pounds
at his temples as he grows furious
lashes at the machine breaks down
the doors howls into the night imploring
the great eye for answers:

                        Hunger gnaws
at the belly of children who listen
to the fluttering of wings of birds
devoid of themselves. They are
the echoing voices of the departed
who live under ash and snow
and wait for the birth of just man.

PLAYING HOUSE

I am mad chair swivelling above
him drawing out of his belly
voices that speak his cadence
connecting me to the masters
of a wardrobe of song renewed
in the mouth of warm stone
rhythms that wane and do not wane.
Inside the moon is
the drum they buried in our sexes
perfect fit for a universe
where man and I play house.

MY MAN LOSS

One day loss moved into my body
grew limbs hands with fingers to press
at my heart metal fingernails to poke
at my insides. Long rattling sounds
rose with the snake at the core of my veins
growing heavy with all those dead.

Burdened by itself loss moved
into the house of dream. Once there
it began to appear to me nightly
attired in black suits, assuming other
personalities for my crumbling occasions.

One dark night loss sat at my desk
began to write about a long corridor
beneath the foundations of my house
there where gauze covered the skeletons.

I sat on the knees of loss pointed
to silence, spoke to him about my country
its rivers its dependencies its amphibious
tongues that enter leave the drawers
of these dark furnishings.

Time has passed. Sorrow now
has me bound to the tree of
childhood whose limbs grow inward.

Etched on bark, loss's face appears,
his eyes return to their sockets his mouth
still detached speaks to me of days
spent frightening the predators in
the woods where we finally are, I his
Rapunzel, he my Knight, insomniac
and alone with his detached body parts.

FREAK SHOW

We meet man I and our
retinue of shadows
at public functions
where the length of love
is discussed by others.

Long sessions.

The words
fall exhausted
at our feet.

A special panel on the theory
of whispers sews man and me
to the spines of large tomes
which are to be ground
on the archival
stone where our lives
are put to the test.

I beseech him to leave
the conference floor and
join me inside dioramas
where prairie grasslands and summer
breezes extend our moist breath
insufflating life into the
king and queen who live
with our other selves.

Mark Laba

ZEIGLER'S CORAL REEF

god was bourbon
and knife-thin knees
staggering around with
a nose for appearances and a lust
for dimly lit motor courts
in the spring.

doors were opening to obese hosts
limping and thrusting toothbrushes
at the nerve endings of BBQs,
shrubs thumping with
unhealthy reports.

behind the camera
it was all shankless picnic pork shoulders and
kooky coital clutches.

kiss of the oarblade
made out my name
slime deep in innocence and
hissing furniture.

the body is an open vessel,
the brain full of phantom wormings
and the lungs on the lookout
for pocket change.

DUCK PONDS OF BERLIN

it was a long afternoon.
safety deposit boxes
sat in armchairs
and joked about the heat
perspiring like tourists
cramming luggage into motel rooms.

the air was so garbled
it bubbled from its skin
and telepathy fell on the forearms
of public figures
drizzling blood into well-worn slippers.

speaking about events
his wife found him dead
at half past one
although he appeared to be
sweeping the steps
and with his left foot
he imitated a starving frog.

nevertheless, they duplicated the story of a king
who thought he was a clock
but was not, lost on a conveyor belt
of dangerous digestion, listening constantly
for the ominous bong
of forceps striking the glockenspiel.

SPONGE BATH

Helmet of thick
　　forebodings,
　　dropping from the trees
　　　bobbing and weaving,
　like goggle-eyed voices
　　strapped to torpedoes.
　　he cleans his own shoes
　　and his daughter is rumoured
　　　　to have a beard.
　They descend in a
　　crude bucket,
　the reservoir filled with the
　　humped backs of their neighbours,
　　　brutal bedchambers opening onto
　　terraces filled with
　　clucking tailors and the blind snap of
　　　moustaches creating fire from
　　ornamental driftwood.
　　　they called for the gallstone-maker,
　　slumbering like a great cheese danish
　　　or the death of the Christian martyrs,
　　　stamping with debauched hoofs
　　on a variety of clots and
　　　　roadways,
　　the warbling song
　　　like bedroom slippers
　　shuffling helplessly on a tennis court
　　　at dawn,
　　hands cupped and
listening for the luggage of strangers.

TALES FOR SALESMEN

I wobble
on blood-vessel stilts,
bobbing over shredded wheat
like dowagers kissing offspring,
knee-deep in pay toilet grunts.

Remember, thick is the forest where the breakfast termites
          dig their graves,
and don't be surprised
if they look like
Arthur Godfrey,
pop-eyed
and covered in illustrations of ice bags.

So I boiled the water,
added the nose, lungs and
skin,
building vagrancy
on the installment plan,
honeymooning
with mannequins
and generally
taking the fun
out of
mountaineering,
barking and parking
cars
with my aquatic technique.

Don't spray peanuts at me,
my unforeseen anatomy doesn't knock,
it rings these days
with a nervous voice answering
to say, "Mr. Dudley is not home,

he committed suicide
with a dead pig
out at Moose Lake."

A poor man was making hats
    so I explained something
        to him.
 "I'm the Pullman car killer
  with no marbles
  and couple'a liquor stores
    for the
  wandering Jews.
    Next time you pass
 my house
  I expect some centre of
    gravity
  and a glass of
  whiskey."
Who knew?

Drycleaning, lightbulbs, lobster-stained
pyjamas, the chuckle in my voice
takes 750 muscles and the hair on
my head
is your only
down payment.

STUBBY'S LUAU

Someone sent him
a letter
  written on a
  shrimp cocktail...
It said,
  "under a microscope
    they named a town
    after you
  and in this town
    no asparagus
      is served
      in the restaurants."

Strange bedfellows
and the snoring of
meatballs.

Me
and a million other
  jerks
  were whiskey-soured into needless
    brain surgery,
  bankrupt magicians
    fitting us for tuxedoes.

An empty stomach
  stuck a knife in me.
  Now I take three olives
    with my martini
  and all the curves
    I can fit in a straitjacket.

Covered by funeral expenses
I'm looking like

a million bucks
  taking a long nap
   on a short stick
     of dynamite.

Salted peanut Napoleon eyewash.
And I had my loan approved at the lemonade stand.

I drive
the buggy
   of money
through a variety of
social circles,
  fully subpoenaed and shining
   with the future
     of a European
       cabbage.

I'm a heart attack
trying on a
  new suit, though
  I'm old enough
  to be my own
passport photo.

On Monday the hula dancers
   entered the machine
  and by Tuesday
  they were on a waterbed
   in Florida
  pressing infections between
  the waffle irons.

 I smoke my breakfast
  into a grave appearance,
  for eighty years

I owned a revolving door
on Lake Michigan
and the drinks wore
  tight shoes
around an expired parking meter.

"I heard your daughter is a sword-swallowing onion dancer
on an estate in Reno where she's expecting a new coat and
a tree surgeon in wash-and-wear pants."

Imagine that.

That's it,
  that's my report card.
Even the florist can't complain,
  built on the solid
  grandmothers of executive signatures,
drenched in laryngitis
  and eyes screwed to the wall like
   crash landings.
My soup's cooling,
my toothpick railroad finished,
  this is my hair net,
  this is what the dentist charges,
these are my pets, my razor and tuba,
  this is the blueprint
  for my bread and butter,
   for frankfurters,
 for the conveyor belt in the
    shopping centre,
  party's over,
  pig's asleep
   and I'm under the sink
  kissing capillaries and wearing
  a life jacket.

LOVE PLAN

Want to spend my dough
   any way I want to?
Whose deadly blade called Peking at my request?
 No soap but there were punchbowls
and steel fingers with fools' names flexing with their weight.
    Honour me in my wretched home
   clean as a whistle with
   singed hair,
  fat, squishy lawnchairs and a gunsight
   in the mirror.
That's the name of
  this charter member,
  complex-ridden, peanut-filled
  and a gallows
  from top to bottom.

PALM BEACH STORY

Miami
and her tales of chopping wood,
   about arm's length
  and hinged on peculiar
  souvenirs.
  Stickpin alibis
  and a steady fist
   grinding fleas
   into apartment carpeting.
   A fat man sweating
two-handed pinochle
   near a rotting palm and
sympathy
smoking cash
down to
   a push-button musical.
   In the medicine cabinet
  mouths dropped like
  an airstrip
generating suspicion.
  And the
  proud citizens
  bound by glowing chamberpots
  were ready for
  a pig's tusk
  of two-fisted adventure
with the lunkhead
behind the six gates
   of dusk.

THE MISER'S LAMENT

A couple of industrious insects stopped for drinks.
"I've learned my lesson," said Tiny thumbing bills like a millionaire
        giving a sucker an even break.
Around them the
songs of birds
dirty and sordid and the
tidal pull
of factory chicken.
Warming the eyes
with panic.
"That's some wild oats," said Uncle Bread,
vigorated from his camphor rubdown,
spitting hotel rope
from retail teeth
and blowing smoke rings
with the stiffs.
It was a shack job,
a man-trap
pimpled with shameless bowling alleys,
money invested
in a filthy tongue
and a dog driving taxi
in Minneapolis.
Eggs, bacon and swivel chair snorting
and an inventory that could embroider
blackmail like cocktails
on your peripheral vision.
Call me old-fashioned with my geese in swimsuits,
a light lunch, some Swiss hocks and then the
intercom spoke.
"You know what, friend?" it said.
"After this no more hissing of proctologists."

LEARN MAGIC

Supply me with cakes and ale,
hot buffet veins
and a parking space
for my half-cocked knuckles
and seeing-eye muggings.
Knobless
I walk the halls
unbuttoning my baboon
and palpitating a caboose.
Stop in at the secretary pool,
put a few bets on
the gilded hearse,
then move to the keyhole
and slip my voice into
a wallet.
Ventriloquist spit drips
from a sullen stethoscope,
dummy's heartbeat
pumps fresh drinks for the audience
and my head vanishes
among the neckties of
the tired barbers of the midwest,
turning seaward towards
a darkened lobby.

Lance La Rocque

A BODY OF KNOWLEDGE

i

Learning is like drowning
in your own body
lingering in its waves
rolling into rocks

ii

they're there like spears and bombs
in your own body,
the eyes locked from behind —
two world portals closed

iii

for the season: descend,
in your own body.
Sounds re-sound in the dark —
its own quality

iv

of light erupts here too
in your own body
rippling over its scars
sliding into sores.

v

This is where you camp out?
In your own body?
And at night with no fire?
Night and a river

vi

where the bears gravitate
— in your own body —
and the terror of it,
for once, you embrace.

HERE'S HOPING!

I hear you
lady (still)
hold the foetus
jarred
to your breast

glass skin

bobbing in the liquid
like a thing

I'll never be

blind
container
of your dreams.

LOCUS OF THE SOUL

Why not just say —
where do you think
on *your* body
the soul grows?

They all have 'em.
My mother's is on her nose,
its   intense   active   broken   arc
axing the sky
I see through
1963 to forever.

Mine squats in my stomach.
Hunched shoulders
conceal it from your
nosey gaze, look
the soul!

likes stomachs.

I wish mine had grown up
deep in the musculature — so solid.
Alert. It would ripple through space,
hardwired for murder — all the
mobs of eyes!
All these hot, swarming noses!

HISTORY IN THE NEW WORLD ORDER

We might at least lay down
these mirrors on graves
and release our visions.

There's no longer a way to
people
the dead
with the lives
they deserve
again
and
again.
They go out.

Unsmiling corpses. They are
longing for organs
and holes —
           fingernails and
cigarettes. It is time.

I need a mad, fierce flame here
to pour over our machinery.

It goes out.

A JAR OF CHICKENS (LEECHING)

I'll take my chickens
in a jar, no cans please, because
I like to see just
what it is
I'm eating   inside
how a chicken floats.
Jars.
Within the deep turquoise
glow emanating from in the glass —
it's the chickens' making
for some irretrievable space
their strange escaping colours
of the sagging earth.

UNDERSTONES

The grass root tangles
laces place,
paths, pockets   open/shut
of dark   fabric
dreaming
guts of the earth

I WANNABE / REPO MAN

I come across a field
of ears
blowing about trees like leaves
and a noiseless wind was

dumb torture
deaf earth.

I myself have no limbs to speak of,
arms, legs, fill in the blanks, the lot...
that if I can call my own
legally, at least,
I am leased
a nominal head
earless, eyeless — less — so to speak

dispersed along the landscape
the ears tossed
by a forest thick
w/ amputated hands and
arms, legs, the lot...
disperse

tongue
spirits tied and get tired are
and *I am*
by some definition

dumb torture
deaf earth.

INFINITY

for Dubya

Just before
the end of things,
I saw them:

butterflies! butterflies!
swarming! swarming!
through
the stomach of the world.

MOON:

fat-bellied spider —
legs
must be clothed
in clouds

A NOVA SCOTIA LOVE STORY

The blackflies graze
in clots along
my arms and legs.

HISTORY IS THE EXCEPTION

This present
is this
present.
The other ones
are sleeping,
their eyes red with
dreaming.
Or not.

The others: imaginary skeletons
deprived of bodies,
writhing under
the linoleum. The asphalt.
The earth.
Or not.

I awaken to this.

Most things are
never born.

But some things are/
born dead.
And ghostlike,
they make their ways
among the furniture,
wandering on the brink
of resignation and despair.

THE CROWS HAVE WINGS AND EYES FOR WATCHING LOVE

I tried to take her
under my wing
but found there
was only arms, small and white,
weak and thin
for everyone to see them
pretending to be wings —
fluttering around me
and her
with knowing grins and claws, they

await the predictable
birth of shocked eyes.

6 MONTHS / 40 YRS

my creature
my little creature
all limbs and
all eyes
how I feel the future like a knot —
going up
and going down
the night stairs of you, unexpectedly,
caught in the throat of a pause.

BOY-MACHINE

When I was a
little girl
was I ever ever
a little bud
with fine feathered petals, little colour birds emergent
and littler
mechanical clasps
strained their necks up
the apparatus and
looking for some luck,
a lock.
It didn't take.
For when it set the
body walk to
a feminine gait
and an arm yanked an arm
"Stop it!", well —

There are surely felt many heaps of
parts and bones sunk cluttering
down in the dark
waters and soil
of the cellars —
machines rehearsing their lines of flight.

Lillian Necakov

HANGING FROM A TELEPHONE WIRE

I

Around midnight the light is fragmented
through the open window troubled cries
I hear footsteps across broken glass
the street lamps are spent
night rushes toward me at an alarming speed
a tired fury occupies the city

II

a procession of coffins winds its way through my streets
spring is a silent witness
a derailed shell of a streetcar lies on its side
wounded and forgotten
the smell of crocuses and gasoline mingle
conjure the memory of indulgence
a pair of shoelaces hanging from a telephone wire
the only mourners left

III

in one of those corridors jackboots and nightsticks
do a dance
breathless smokestacks point to the heavens
marring the possibility of innocent sky
we are all carriers of savagery
infected with the ceremony of war

IV

history is sometimes overruled
revenge jump-starts the spirit
reason enough to get out of bed
to cross to the other side of the river
kneel before the enemy
then press his head against a stone wall
making him listen to the centuries of rage
that haunt the landscape

V

helicopters hover over the sacred ground
dark-haired women crawl along its surface
their long fingers plucking bullets out of the dirt
after sundown they will sing their children to sleep
between songs in hushed voices they will recite
the make and calibre of weapon that carried each bullet

VI

wet newspapers cover the sidewalk
we march down the street trying not to look down
but the rain gives us no choice
there is no escape from the chronic recognition
of words

VII

there are laws of gravity
laws of war
oppression
authority
struggle
day
night
suspicion

VIII

what we demonstrate against
is the part of us that once made us whole
the tiny speck of complacency once allowed
our gift is buried in the outskirts of town
courage is a rare bird
there is nothing left to talk about

IX

a man with a camera stands on a rooftop
takes a picture of a wounded dog
someone begins hurling rocks
we lie facedown in the garden for hours

X

we put our hands into vulnerable pockets
pulling out something shiny
a gold tooth with an inscription
"this is the price we pay for facing east when we pray"

2F AVE. CHICAGO

for Richard Huttel

he went and did it
unhinged himself
split the seam between his shoulder blades
sprouted wings
buried his cold soup in the garden
and blew one long hard note on his imaginary saxophone

but you know what?
I'm pretty sure I heard it
all the way down by the pond
some kind of zen jazz

I didn't even notice the frozen faces
in the ice below me
as I skated to the notes
carried on a stolen wind.

MUNICH – PARIS

After Werner Herzog's "Of Walking in Ice"

Monday

a stout waitress in a tractor
pointing to a schoolhouse
examines my boots
a Spanish priest plays pickup sticks
in the snow
his robes flapping against the howling wind
an epileptic crow

absurd little blessing
my journey makes sense

Tuesday

Lotte is alive
if I walk
she is alive

in this village a girl pushes a frozen bicycle
across the meadow
later
when I am not looking
I know she will lick the ice off the spokes
and I will be forced to tell the truth

Wednesday

every road is ugly
every river is guilty of something
blue smoke billows from tiny cottages in the distance
I am surrounded by November
moving moonstruck
into the barking night

Thursday

a dog is sniffing a rainbow
that is lying across the broken train tracks
I rest in a ditch
this is where the Gestapo once marched
I pull out my comic books
the ones with the good guys

it is still miles away

Friday

cheerless Turks
sucking on sugar cubes
stare as I pass through their streets
women behind birdcages giggle
the absurdity of my journey implies
that I am not dreaming

dusk settles
I have been poisoned by loneliness

Saturday

on the edge of Paris
a dead zebra draped across a fountain
catching my breath
I am tempted to piss in the street

Sunday

she is alive
someone had telephoned
told her to wait

and when I walked into her room
I was jealous
of how blissfully she had taken to the illness

I did not tell her the truth *then*
I sat with her
while the radio carried on.

ART DISEASE (A TRANSLATION)

The conductor's ensemble of tendencies
requires frequent submission

like Duchamp's autograph — which accompanied him to the orange
        pyramids —
we use a different syntax

the quail image results in an iron tourist cliché
such as the venetian blind

snow is very enigmatic
while we explore the delicatessen

when we wash *that* brand of paper, a falcon appears

sculpture resists difficulty in the bathing violin

the vulgarizer of photographs elaborates a dictionary
a fatal joy is etched across the sky

the surgical utensils defend the comparison

resenting the object produces change.

DAMAGE

Under broken semaphores
in a birdless city
muzzled, forgotten, veiled and tortured
we are bent by hatred

while we kiss the feet of a mute girl by the side of the road
the origin of our thirst is drowned by a cargo of rotting vowels
day follows night and then again night
and so it goes
yesterday's bones are already archived and forbidden
there is dust
the taste of birth, faint on our tongues
where we once waited for god
the transgressors perform the executioner's song in morse code
the echo of hunger is captured
in a broken jar somewhere in the desert.

THE TWELVE SPIRITS OF CHAOS

1. Know that every day is an opportunity for transformation

lick her flesh with the end of a live wire until her metal nerves
cause the changing of the seasons
wipe your mouth clean
then refresh her memory of how it used to be

2. Hear the voice from above

listen to Joe Strummer and Joey Ramone one more time
before they turn on the war

3. Understand that we are all mirrors

his intention is desire but the accident will occur in the corridor
as he unbuttons your shirt he is confronted with the tragedy
of a very foreign landscape
the scalpel is not so cold against your nipples

4. Trust the creator

close your eyes tight, right at the top of the hill
pedal as fast as you can
whispering gratitude
whispering "holy magnet"
then listen

5. Ask for divine assistance

choking on the juices of a ripe moon you realize the darkness
your bones begin to come undone
the efforts of a single firefly against the monumental absence of light
cause you to fall to your knees begging for sickness

6. Realize that we are all being tested

after you have trampled your neighbour's lilac bushes
lick the ink drops off the dining-room table
coach your children to use scissors
for editing the world

7. Repent with joy

I think this means:
going down the highway smiling is a good thing
after you have run over a dog

8. Be never satisfied

clean the barn over and over

9. Walk like the blind

when you stick a needle in your arm make sure it is made of pure silver
allow the mercury to ooze slowly into your veins
then step into the traffic (you will find this is akin to falling in love)

10. Use death as a motivation

if you look out your window and see a horizon of voodoo dolls
accept the dance

11. Experience the pain as our own

on enemies, use only the kinds of weapons
you would want used on yourself

12. Don't judge others

forgive the man who was caught kissing the volcano
his disfigured lips are his final mistress

FISSION

When I was born
my brother howled, purple-faced
in the courtyard

that was before our great migration
while the galaxy still rippled
faint traces of godliness across her face
before she understood
that we would outlive her
and become a bundle of cordless monkeys
under a roof of miscarried stars
falling one by one into our sleeves.

Stuart Ross

AN ORPHAN

An orphan stands on a balcony singing something that would become popular in the next century. His papa takes notice, and licks him with a tongue of flame. An office building blows by, hugged in the arms of a schoolgirl. The roiling clouds assume the shape of a giant eyeball and gaze down approvingly.

A spider hides in an ashtray, trembling amid the cigarette butts. An orphan lies on the sofa, coughing and sweating, clutching the channel-changer. In the kitchen, a miracle occurs in the fridge, then goes back to normal. First the curtains are sucked out the window, then everything else.

Aroused after crawling such a long way, a mirror french-kisses a dirty puddle. The sign above the billiards hall begins to sneeze, for all the chalk. An orphan sees his mama in the eye of a baked potato, the eye of a baked potato. A cry breaks free from a plastic bag.

A production of *The Mikado* is cancelled because none of its cast is human. The legs of a bed are peppered with mosquito bites. An act of desperation flosses its teeth, trying to look its best for church. An orphan buries an abacus on a beach beside an empty ocean.

A TRAUMATIC HIGH SCHOOL TAP-DANCING INCIDENT

The detectives found an unusual
substance on the walls and sniffed
each other's shoes and ears. The principal
shivered in his office, clutching the trophy
he won for public speaking three
decades earlier. The janitor, a prostitute
with a heart of gold, incinerated
absolutely everything and invited us
to watch it burn. A window slammed shut
on the second floor
and broke Sheldon Teicher's fingers.
His teacher screamed. A beaker
fell to the floor and exploded.

But here's what I wanted to tell you:
Miriam Cohen and Hedy Cohen,
who were not sisters, not even
related, were practising
for the big presentation,
their taps in sublime synchronicity,
when Mr. Cohen, who was
one of them's father,
shouted through the window
from out in the parking lot:
something about
a baloney sandwich
with mustard.

YANKEE DOODLE

I

What hopper be uttered has been uttered face to face:
To that end, the bards withhold, unruffled.
They swoop and attack the pristine raucous.
Somebody kennels his noggin against the banquette.
Moreover you, in a flabby falsetto, implore their nudges
Into the gloaming. He restrains kennelling his noggin.
Thing is you, which are disastered,
Plop fuzz over and above him.
Thing is therefore you stirred up,
The creature infatuated, the gore shampooed from the train.
The darkness's lingering venom, permissive and smooth,
Has goaded her blister. Thirsty times that I have beheld:
      Stagnant, protracted,
Released in absolute strife, the tenuous props unripe.
Or, gavaged on odium, she pickles the tingle
Of else's distress; perchance the fiendish
Betrothed of a poxen or noodle.
I suffer from no offspring. I request no one.

II

The blushing glims of bunnies
Aren't deplorable. Dead person outstrips
The deplorable precious dorp in a tender
Unlimited encore. Supposing the secrecy droops alop;
It is dead person's vice.
Thereabouts and thereabouts and thereabouts,
High and low the identical honk
Of tortures obtainable, and gadgets
Sprouting ancestors, sprouting
Speechless. Supposing the pooches
Glitter blushing, that's

Jackstraw's pursuit. The bunnies
Will empty their wisdom.
Near midday in the defect a throbbing skink
Hovered for drama, its jostles rapt,
Guarding the crook of a fussy incursion.
Ripe to a modulation, the jostles hovered.
The workers bagged violent on the defect.
Troll skeletons rambled the wags.
And yon were additional passwords
That euthanasia sparked us, by beverage, sparked us
By pasture: between the laments
An unfrizzled snake that rotated against agar–agar
Rumped in the dirty vapour.
Blood, not euthanasia, is the rigorous ruin.

III

The climax utterly
Snares the señorita, extinguishing her
Psyche in a hairdo of transport
That broadcasts by means of her aggregate soma.
Her jittery, hot-blooded, and sinewy
Isms share in the edict.
The strengths of the basin engage
And bounce a hydrant of gum from the neck
Whereas the sinewy, sipping petitions of the neck
Assist the vestibule of the seed.

NEW HOPE FOR THE DISENFRANCHISED

It was at that exact moment, when
I began to empty my pockets,
which were empty to begin with,
except for a bent paperclip
and a tennis court oeuf (an
athletic and popular omelette,
sprinkled with pocket lint),
that my children returned from the future,
from long after my sorry death,
where they were quite comfortable and,
I was happy to hear,
saw each other often and spoke of me
not unkindly, if infrequently.
"I was just emptying my pockets,"
I told them, "liberating myself
from all things material, but look,
let's go to the zoo!" "The zoo!" they cried.
As we ambled among the apes,
my eldest, whose name I no longer
remember, gone from my noggin
along with my own, said to me,
"Everything's different later on.
A guy got shot
and hubbub ensued,
but when the dust settled, Dad,
it was a whole other thing."
Flanked by lemurs and ostriches,
I gathered my children
within the arc
of my fatherly arms.
I knew now that after I croaked,
a guy would get shot
and all would be better.
With the penguins looking on,

and under the gaze of giant turtles,
I kissed each of my children
(it took nearly an hour) upon
their foreheads, and I set off
for home. I had children
to conceive, a blender to fix,
rectangular books
to return to the library.

THE SUN

after Georg Trakl

The sun wears the blue sky like a hospital gown.
The deer are shadows among the trees.
The man doesn't know whether to torture or nurture.

The insects skid across the pond's surface.
The earth expands and contracts.
The boat is sleepy, but it is also hungry.

Earthworms caress the corn's narrow roots.
The great mouth of night stretches wide.
A swan confronts a killer.

The planets open their moist white eyes.
The wanderer's legs are one hundred and heavy.
A flash of light tears a hole in the night.

SUEÑO PERDIDO

after Valery Larbaud

Oh endless gray clouds choking the sky,
black moon, invisible stars,
distant squeal of tires beneath
the shell of a car with a tree growing through it;
oh various trembling monsters
that lurch through cold empty cellars,
and whose scribbled claws swipe from beneath my bed,
who await me in places I'll never go; oh
constant clatter of locomotives through
my chest, tiny trembling pigeon
lodged in my bowels, ill-formed kernels of love
glittering in the back of my throat,
in my shoulders, in the palms of my hands;
oh vivid memories of decades before my birth,
of all the pain I've caused, and the pain for which
I bear no blame, the peaceful dreams
of those dear to me, the misspellings on
eroded headstones shrouded in mist; oh chaos,
exhaustion, bliss, confusion, serenity, blankness,
panic, quiet, quiet;
oh endless roaring clouds
rolling over my head, I offer you this:
my lost sleep.

A GUY, SOME FLIPPERS, A BUILDING

He got his flippers on
and it made him go swimming.
It was tough, but he kept on swimming.
Then he saw the water was pavement
and he remembered his grandpa's words:
"Pavement is the hard one.
You don't need your flippers for it."
He racked his brains to recall
what "don't" meant and meanwhile
he bumped his head into a building.
A building's a square thing with a hole inside
where people live or maybe work.
Inside the building that bumped his head,
a woman made copies of a sheet of paper
with words on it, and while she made copies
she thought about a river
and the way she could float on her back
on top of it, on the part where it met the air.
Above, the sky was crammed with clouds.
A bird was a dark thing in it.

EXPERIMENTS ON ORAL SUCTION AND GILL BREATHING IN FIVE SPECIES OF AUSTRALIAN TADPOLE

I slept encased in the cement of the balcony.
A chimp lay nestled in each of my nostrils.
In the apartment above, a man read the last rites
to his TV set, and in the apartment below,
the screeching of lusty raccoons in the shower.

"Remember the days," she said, "when we met?
You wore a white smock
and plucked your gray eyebrows."
Far above her piled-up hair, two planets collided,
and civilizations were gone in an instant.

A head becomes full with too many regrets.
A bead of a chemical hangs from a dropper.

ALWAYS HAPPEN IN A DUSK

The sun goes away.
Shivering commences.
Cheap love in a house ensues.
A tree bends over from the wind.

Cancer is a baddy.
We got muscles in us now.
Parents look after the little ones.

A raccoon lights a cigarette.
Now I must rest on a pillow.

Steve Venright

FLOORS OF ENDURING BEAUTY (Selections)

There is a white stiffness breathing out the murk from a sullen plethora of chapels in that same seaside town. A candycane of moody regrets is what the fish are jumping for, right near the shore. Unbeknownst, even to us, we walk in terry-cloth silence upon the sooty beach as the lighthouse bursts into artificial flame. Please save these sailors, O wretched leviathan that lives within our dreams. They're decent pure souls who are in it just for the money, though they've every one come to love what they do. Let their bodies wash up to shore where we will mend their clothes and watch in talented horror as the locomotives roar right out of the waves and blast the beach with their predatory roar. Vicious radiance! The night collapses in our throats.

§

You and your prairie of voices, with stripes that excite me. Furry skyscrapers stand camouflaged in wheatfields. Farmers circumnavigate them in combines at night — deep silent night where the dead thrive. But this is no subject for a snowy urban afternoon. Let's talk about the woodgrain of floorboards and fluid dynamics instead. And squid, if you don't mind.

§

They killed a moose whereas he's just posing in the mineral gallery with his juror's cap. One eye on the outside world, one eye on the crenellated ooze that remains unvacuumable. Sitting on a terrace in France without benefit of seaways or arches, envious of men who kiss trophies in public. The news is all about a giant toad named Die Knoblauchrote — goes around eating owls that fall from trees after he hypnotizes them. A toddler on the tracks in a poster for the Sharpened Dance. You can't come within a mile of the smiling people without there being a chance operation. Is she a girl or a world or someone else's intention? Swans are screwing in the artificial pool. It's a closed system, enabling them not to die. It doesn't stop them from decaying, though. After several decades, you can imagine the state of their hair, not to mention the estate of their heir who went off and dyed a head of them. *There's a pretty face,* they'll say, *and she's a doctor of degeneration!* The speakers were all uninvited and none of them showed up. They blare their grolly horns from the debts of their disparity, where no one else has been, save for the three goats watching television in the nude. Without benefit of spatial cognition, without recourse to freeways and sanatoriums, I no longer care about her perfect collarbones, her distinguished uvula, her incomparable noise floor.

§

Nerves turn to powder here — didn't anyone mention? — but there's a silken jelly you can use that gets them back to almost normal. They sell it down at the wildlife organarium behind the prison. It's good for sliding scales, too.

§

They put up false archways to scare the horses. They also offer prizes for loud lovemaking in tombs. My current theory is that something crawled up into the motor and died there.

On this night the cows sleep more deeply than usual. The ice cubes are melting in my nightcap. A lodge is being demolished. What else? Oh yes: when I said there were things I hadn't told you, I was lying to conceal a deeper truth. This is the ditch where everything coalesces into pure burning senseless reason. It's my sanctuary and it's sinking with a grim dissonant beauty. Your forgiveness is like a new egg to me. I jump on it from the overpass.

§

Bowls for vomiting oracular data, holographic but strong. The little Ming girl does her regurgitory duty then rides her triossicle over the fucking alligators. Her restrained delight is obviously ancient and afflicts the crowd, most of whom have apparently never been to a museum of this nature.

Show us firewinds twirling in the heartland. Show us clay pigeon circuit boards blasting over coastal resorts. Let there be a great sucking sound as the bland ones are lifted upwards. And there's a bar full of saints where Vitas dances nightly and Anthony sits confabulating madly on a stool. It's mainly because of the meat but it's also because there's a new phoenix tomb smoking between every word.

§

In a blaze of chocolate the wood nymph hurtles through the office tower, exciting tensions and defoliating zeitgeists. We follow her with remote-control cameras, down to where the grocers lay their eggs. It's a creaky salvation for one who held the floor with quicksilver statuary not months before the arrest of those dark corporate rangers. I look out from a static breeze and catch a glimpse of hell: trowelled sarcophagi unlit in the sulphurous dawn, pricks hanging out at the stock exchange, overpriced steamed zucchini. All I want is to park my cats and call it a day. But the foam is up to my ankles now, and the clouds are down to my neck. I can hear the police in the alley crying out for sleep. It's a good sound.

§

I see something packing itself into a Citroën, with gassy ligatures and shallow water tucked under infatuated seams. There are good-looking fish here and scapular glissandos fighting to free us from the white and silver dome. Mouth scaffolding appears in rogue outskirts pulled into night like a magician's handkerchief through an unclosed wound arriving in 1982 or thereabouts.

So your theory was true: it is possible to cakewalk without hydroscopes; it is possible to scour the faucets without using animal products. And why would we want to pay for animal products when we can support our own economy? Let's proceed based on the hypothesis that certain frequencies can slump through unplunged slivers of crawling solar flares. Nothing would change — you and I would still be represented by ciphers, there would still be trashy hoards of dizzy bards dashing abroad aboard dachshunds on dashboards flashing forward into new upheavals, new revelatory quests, new standard effects.

Anything begets everything. The voices in the background are part of the music. The ticket booth is part of the performance. The war is an advertisement. The candies are stuck in the grate. Sloops in spools and archaic ivory waltzes performed without breath in serious calm places. Palaver caverns. Glottal dales. Whitewashed hells burning through our wires like a vain model, an architectural template of ovoid steel. The noise behind the curtain is part of the tour. Let it guide you down poured concrete chasms into the secret lush interior of the soft core populated by gorgeous demons who couldn't care less about you. Let it take the form of a golden cocoon, a crinkled origami raccoon that bites at your postulations and frivolously entices porcupines the size of the moon held out at arm's length. Thus will you be led into the antechamber. A moiré eel. Start to chop it into pieces with your tongue. They will arraign you according to sighs.

SIX EPISTLES (Excerpts)

To Capt. Ganzfeld
c/o Glidding Meadows Airport

Dear Captain Ganzfeld,
I'm a big fan of yours. I can't believe the way your guffling plumes
have inflected our airways. There are messages flatulated by each
froompy jet you pass in — the sound means the same as the vapour
trail interpreted. My mother says it's coincidence. At first I wasn't that
interested. Anyone can scar the skyflesh in a Messerschmitt or Spitfire,
and just because the jets are now supersonic at times doesn't mean
they're less of a nuisance. But that nuisance, I began to realize as I
developed into a girl (what I was before, they won't tell me), was
becoming a *new sense* of possibility. Your gorgeous jets quickly became
my reason for living, superseding hippopotami (too long to explain).
While you were up there concocting aerial soufflés, I was down
here on the roof of the greenhouse scratching away because of an
unremitting skin condition — it flakes off in chunks, down to raw
underness, but grows back even better. Still — can you imagine —
they actually put one of those dog cones on my head so I couldn't
claw the sides of my face too easily. What shitty embarrassment!
But the upside of it was that your cumuloid arias were even more
pronounced and better articulated to my ear than they had been
before the imposition of the cone. Yes, I was scratching away quite
heartily when it occurred to me that you could be getting a much
wider audience for your work. Since that time, I have been controlling
you telepathically. Nothing too extreme, mostly just the repetition of
certain ravishing patterns and blossoming frumpages. Now, I'm not an
educated person: my aunt on my father's side speaks every fourth word
and my uncle on my mother's side speaks every word all the time and
it's sadly been damaging to him. Great clumps he can't help spewing
out — his mouth is broken now and he's unable to keep anything in.
Before the onset of his concretic logorrhoea, he was a wizard among
dermatologists, and I'm sure he's my only hope of restitution. I have
long pleaded for his help and he now says he'll cure me if you'll cut

out that racket. He's quite willing to go fist to fist with you, but I tell him you're not that kind of man. I even tell him you're not that kind, and that you're not of man. Still, he wants to at least go sword to toe with you. All he does is watch television all day. He says it energizes him and nourishes his lunar plexus. Now, personally I think that you could take him. But supposing you succeed — there'll be no one to remove my affliction. On the other hand if you lose, well, we've lost one of the great artists of our age. Here's my solution: you stay up there in your dainty black jets and then, while he levitates during a commercial break, I will let the air out of him. He'll become a sheet I can fold and lay as a healing blanket across my indentations. If all of this sounds a bit convoluted, I apologize. I just wanted you to know how deeply I admire what you do and when you do it, but that you may be in just a bit of trouble because of the foregoing implication. If at any time you want the spell broken — my remote-control spell, I mean — just say these words and you'll plummet like a nest of goslings worn as a hat by a woman who's just been struck by a bail of hay. I know, you're probably wishing by now that you'd never heard from me. I thought it important, however, that you realize your actions are largely due to impulses of my imagination. It is only because I care very deeply for you, and because I have ivy growing on my leg cast, that I am confessing these things. It will not explain the lizards in your bath water — they're largely metaphorical, I suspect — but it will give you some insight into why you've flown over my urban farm seven times in the last hour alone. My mother thinks it's because of a neurological condition. Do I flatter myself too much to dream that it might be something more? Something outside either of our control? And yet, love is a neurological condition, isn't it. It grows on the sides of buildings and they chop it down. But our love, I fantasize, would be different. Your frowzy manoeuvring will eat through my disease and the flowers planted there will blossom in your image. I cannot say more without kissing your fuselage. I cannot betray you, but it looks as though — despite my scheme — a duel of some sort may be inevitable. I'm getting tired of writing this wretched letter to you. I can't even remember what the point of it was now. Also, cracks have begun to form in the ceiling, and it sounds like there are ungodly things giving birth up there. Please make your jets go sweetly, and kick up a little extra rumpy flamboyance on this next pass. We'll never bring our ancestors back from the dead unless you roar like the prince of swords you are. There's just no simple answer. Everything has its consequences. I guess I'll just sleep on it. No one else is. And when I close my eyes a dog barks. So there you have it: we've come full circle, and beyond that it's all cheap photographs and dried-up froth.

Lasciviously,
Velocity

§

Stuart Ross
Chief Groomer
Proper Tails Pet Salon

Dear Mr. Ross,
The poems you ordered have at last arrived at our warehouse and will be shipped immediately pending your approval. We think you will find these pieces — in the "surrealistic" genre — to be well-crafted and of a generally high calibre. Regrettably, however, one of the poems sustained some slight damage during transportation from our factory in Thedford to our warehouse in West Toronto. The poem in question is the one we ourselves had recommended in response to your interest in "something anecdotal with a high verb count, not too dirty" — the pastoral-flavoured "Frickitt's Curve" (ITEM #10485). Only two short segments have been affected, and not necessarily, I might venture, for the worse. The phrase intended to read "amber-gloved clothesline pole erectors" now reads "taffy-coloured birdbath inspectors," and the line ending "hose down the tracks at railway stops" now ends "hoe down the racks at tailor shops." While we believe these flaws to have resulted from careless handling during transit, we're investigating the possibility that the employee who produced this piece failed to abide by our plant's strict specifications regarding the proper application of semantic fixative. As none of the other poems suffered similar alterations, we cannot rule out this theory.

Having already kept you waiting longer than we should have liked, it will be our pleasure to ship these items free of charge the moment you give us the "go ahead." In addition, we will happily include an additional installment of the modular poem "Floors of Enduring Beauty," as we know from past orders this title is among your favourites manufactured by our company.

On behalf of all of us at TVI, please accept my apology for this incident and know that in future we will do everything in our power to promptly meet your poetry needs. We thank you for your patience and understanding as we eagerly await your reply.

Yours Sincerely,
Roxton Bloor
Customer Service Executive
Department of Poetry and
*   Other Engineered Texts*
Torpor Vigil Industries
Toronto, Ontario

§

To Mr. Khropft and Mr. Polymer
of the Kilchrist Larval Ointment Co.

Gentlemen, I have attained a new glow, and I am convinced it is attributable solely to your tonics. I thank you with all my life and wish the same horrid blessing upon you each.

Yours Lustrously,
Lord Clack

PS: I can't believe my garments alone are making so much noise!

§

Dear Colonel Wive,
My hairdresser has advised me that it would be prudent and auspicious
for me to leave the world at this time. Trusting to your good counsel,
which served me so well during my short apprenticeship with you
at the Wayfarers' Academy prior to your own death, I felt loath to
make any plans regarding this matter without seeking your opinion.
I fully appreciate that there are limitations placed upon you by the
state of non-being vis-à-vis communication with those such as
myself who are, albeit dubiously, among the so-called living;
nonetheless, I am bold and selfish enough to hope that you might be
able to reply for old times' sake with a simple yea or nay, should even
that not prove too difficult or inconvenient. I know that this will not
enhance the probability of a swift response, but I must confess that I
never liked you. In fact, to be perfectly honest, I *dis*liked you. I'll be the
first to confirm that we had some wonderful times together and that, in
all our mediocre yet transcendent dealings, never once did you treat me
in a manner which could be called anything but decent, cordial and
fair. It was just something about you, I guess, and I'm sure it couldn't
have been helped. And yet this little revulsion of mine hasn't stopped
me, after all these comfortable years, from approaching you for a favour
at a time of great personal importance. I will cut to the chase. What I
need desperately to know (to paraphrase the bard) is (to do it again)
this: should I or should I not snuff it?

Now, I don't want to pressure you too much — after all, you
are dead — but if you could see fit to get back to me within four
business days, that would be most congenial to my present spiritual and
financial situation. Never mind why — I know you never cared much
for details. Just answer me, please, to the fullest extent you are capable
within — do I ask too much? — the specified time frame (an interval
which is, my lawyer agrees, quite reasonable). Thank you in advance for

your fiercely conscientious attention to the subject disclosed above by your ardent ex-student and would-be admirer,

Zeddy Thraft, BA

PS: A rat which appeared to bear your features just scampered past my feet as I finished jotting this. Seemed odd — thought I'd mention.

§

L. Rug
Night Wind Dept.,
The Discrete Acquisitions & Deployment Co.

Dear Lester Rug or Similar,
The wombats arrived safely, each in its own decorative encasement. Problem is, I can't tell them apart, they're all so cheerful. Is this typical, or is it just me? Are they indeed separate entities, one from another, or simply biological aliases of one source-wombat? Please respond at your leisure as the situation is not urgent and we're likely to be all dead — I mean, to all be dead! — by the time a communication does arrive. Best of luck with your new position (hope the department lets you keep those "documents").

Hopelessly,
Mogby Rumpidge
Kelpwich Investments

Ginger whacked the cupcakes off the pedestal and Wilmer dragged down the dusty daffodils with his jumbo skewing rod while Catherine suctioned blackbirds from the checkerboard without being too particular about it. Ravagers, in the meanwhile, pillaged the greengrocer's in the guise of pharmaceutical surveyors brandishing scatalytical catapults and we called them "rump hearts." No one other than Keith injured any of the large goldfish or followed his instincts too far. Under the old guard we used to postpone cautioning the flimps (I forget what they are) for hours. Anyone who was anyone came out of the woodwork and shed a tear or tore a shed or rode shotgun against the wind. Manfreda could always be counted on for ingesting the worst brand of manure, so much so that we arranged our appointments around her: taffy-coloured birdbath inspectors came and went, molasses salesmen slithered through the pantry while wetting their trousers and mumbling to the dead, Jackie-Sue's daughter's teacher's dogkiller stalked through the fruit cellar swinging a map turtle on a string, all the while pretending he was back at the office curtailing his secretary, vagrants by the dozen, their sockets blazing, waddled past the scullery window shouting hymn snippets and prices — anyone who wasn't nailed down seemed to transvene upon us in those days. But that was before Harvey started squishing mushrooms through keyholes and Karen, and Melissa started vaselining the retrievers and other short-haired dogs or even dotty spinsters and anybody else who wished to suffer from such slickness. Even church meetings took on a spiritual hue when Reverend Kisspunch began jumping and couldn't stop. Kettie nearly died from laughter and Blain resumed twisting breasts and goiters and whatever else he could find dangling. Precipices lost their meaning. What once was tangled became stretched to such an extent we had to commercialize the riverbeds and hoe down the racks at tailor shops. Great bludgeons occurred, tendrils of exploding moss suffocated us from head to toe but otherwise everything was more or less okay. Screaming faces plastered themselves to the windows of passing trains in verisimilitudes of horror and perhaps alimentary discomfort. Wanda started shooting cats (though I suppose it was in the family). Carlyle ended up in the asylum (but then I guess he was getting paid). And the elderly, come to think of it, began passing away, one by one, in a strange conspiracy of transmigration, leaving us to tend this clumsy world with our own devices.

AFFORDABLE LUXURY

She wore the same outfit two days in a row. The men came and took her away.

§

It comes screaming down the centuries to greet us and we're never home when it arrives.

§

The cat is waiting by a hole in the lawn.

§

We've got enough bombs to blow up the world a hundred times, and yet we don't have the guts to do it.

§

He talks to his basement.

§

They're extracting the joy from children and putting it in stylish energy beverages for hard-working executives.

§

"Pop goes the weasel," I say. "Well don't give it away," she says.

BIOS & STATEMENTS

Editor's Note: I asked the participants in Surreal Estate *to provide me with a biographical note and a statement about their writing, with comments on surrealist influence optional. Originally, I considered engineering some kind of email discussion that I'd include here as an appendix, but this simpler approach makes for an equally lively round-table.*

GIL ADAMSON

PHOTO: ADRIAN ADAMSON

Gil Adamson is the author of two books of poetry, *Ashland* (ECW Press, 2003) and *Primitive* (Coach House Press, 1991), as well as a book of linked short stories, *Help Me, Jacques Cousteau* (The Porcupine's Quill, 1995). Her work has appeared in several anthologies, including *The Last Word* (Insomniac Press, 1995), and in numerous magazines. She lives in Toronto.

My mother used to say that children, poets, and schizophrenics all use language in a similar way. She worked for decades with the mentally ill, and she had kids, one of whom was a poet, so I took her at her word. She felt that schizophrenic speech, no matter how disturbed and hypersymbolic, could be unravelled if you could understand the images in it. The problem was, how do you learn the code if your only informant is crazy? One young man she knew kept talking about a bird. Sometimes the bird was his father, other times it was a bird he'd seen at the zoo, and occasionally inanimate objects were the bird. The only sure thing was that this image meant something to him, and he was trying in vain to tell people about it.

I can, of course, explain what my poems are doing, where the images come from, and what their subjective meanings are, just as I can posit the gross, elemental meanings of my own dreams. It's easy. In fact, it's too easy. We paste conventional meaning everywhere, often where it doesn't belong. For the Surrealists, I gather, dream, imagination, and unconscious thought were sources of truth and moral purity; André Breton even figured they could cure mankind's psychic misery. Okay, that's grandiose, but at least the idea was fresh. To my mind, genuine unconscious thought is pretty hard to access, and it's a painful place for those who live there permanently. Unlike dreams, poems are created consciously, by a person with an ego, at a given point in the person's emotional life. Every poem speaks to those facts. No matter how zealously I may apply the surrealist methods (games, automatism, trying to reside in the imagination), I still know I'm writing something meant to be read by others. Logic enters in, and with it comes pride, trailing like a bad smell.

Though I love the work of Reverdy, Eluard, Arp, I can't claim to know a lot about the history or aesthetic of the Surrealists. Still, I've been able to use elements of surrealism to advance my own method and decontaminate my work. The point, for me, is to start out subjectless. Why? Because the subject inevitably becomes a straitjacket — I tend to overextend metaphors, end with a resounding flourish and, inevitably, the poem bores me. Surrealism thins out my connection to logic and to lyric convention, helps me outrun self-awareness, so the poems maintain (for me) a core of genuine subjective truth. The less I know what the hell I'm saying in a poem, the happier I am with it. Afterwards, of course, I always find the blurred signature of a thesis. In the end, all my poems say *something*. And Breton would approve, I suppose, because like everyone else, he valued communication. Why else write a manifesto?

TARA AZZOPARDI

Tara Azzopardi grew up in the not-so-imaginative suburbs of Toronto. From 1998 to 2000 she published the critically acclaimed *Perpetual Motion Machine Magazine*. In 2001, she and her partner Michael operated and curated the Penny

PHOTO: TARA AZZOPARDI

Arcade Low Art & Print Shoppe — a store dedicated to selling good, cheap art/zines/bric-a-brac and providing good, cheap silkscreening services. Currently, Tara collects junk and continues to draw, paint, write, and make music. One day, she will move to Spain and make movies about unknown (yet underrated) sea creatures.

I really don't know what to say, except that I rarely write. On those rare occasions, I tend to notice some pretty unusual things in the environment around me: photographs of debutantes on the sidewalk, the mayor playing baseball with some rock stars, orphans rioting in Brazil, small animals and insects cursing and smoking. It's amazing what I see.

GARY BARWIN

PHOTO: BENJAMIN BROTT

Gary Barwin (b. 1964) is a writer, composer, and performer. He writes in a range of genres: poetry, fiction, visual and concrete poetry, music for live performers and computers, text and sound works, and writing for children and young adults.

Barwin received a PhD in Music Composition from SUNY at Buffalo. He was the recipient of the 1998 Artist Award from the K.M. Hunter Foundation. Barwin teaches music at Hillfield-Strathallan College and lives with his wife and three children in Hamilton, Ontario, where his bank statements reflect his abiding interest in surrealism.

Publications: *Frogments from the Frag Pool* (poetry with derek beaulieu; The Mercury Press, forthcoming), *Doctor Weep and Other Strange Teeth* (fiction; The Mercury Press, 2004), *Raising Eyebrows* (poetry; Coach House Books, 2002), *Outside the Hat* (poetry; Coach House Books, 1998), *Big Red Baby* (fiction; The Mercury Press, 1998), *Cruelty to Fabulous Animals* (fiction; Moonstone Press,

1995), *The Mud Game* (novel with Stuart Ross; The Mercury Press, 1995), as well as numerous chapbooks, pamphlets (many from his own serif of nottingham editions), picture books for children, and *Seeing Stars*, a young-adult novel.

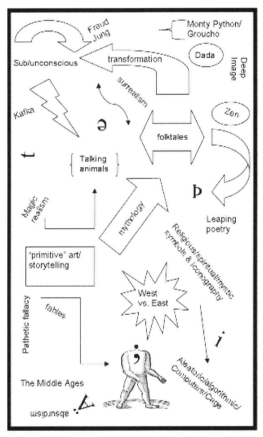

Multiple Listings: An Essay re: *Serial State*
by Gary Barwin

DANIEL F. BRADLEY

i live and work in toronto where i have been active in writing and art since 1984 or so. i have never published a real book by government standards, but i have a number of "biggie smallie books," including (*River of burning movie stars*) (Nemesis Press, 1993), *Books of Blue Frit* (Outlands, 1998), *The Sharp Corners* (The Expert Press, 1999), *poppy sails* (oversion's eternally spinning editions, 2001), *awkward selecter of lowercase swans* (BookThug, 2002), *all sets go* (above/ground press, 2003), and *you will wait for me mid step for my arrival with the slow of arms and fire the ring fingered sky reached come on big boy* (Lyricalmyrical, 2004). over the past decade, my visual work has been included in group shows held in galleries in Toronto. my work has also appeared in a handful of visual poetry anthologies over the years. in 2003 some of my writing was included in the *toronto venezia* anthology, published for an evening in celebration of toronto poetry held in venice, italy. currently i have been listening to a variety of music, including Gustav Mahler, Frederic Mompou, Dmitri Shostakovich, and Bob Wills and His Texas Playboys. i also like film but i love my girlfriend.

over the years, i have explored many different literary techniques in order to find my work. i have worked with suggestions taken from dada, surrealism, haiku, cut-up, concrete, chance, collage, minimalism, and other forms i can't remember. the path i am actively following now is dictation as described by Jack Spicer. by this i mean writing (getting language into paper) the scraps and transmissions i receive from the outside.

my formal education was provided by the ontario public school system. as such it was for the most part useless. however, there were a few teachers who instilled in me a love of art and letters, but their teachings were only seeds that required further education i had to provide for myself. it took a long time to bear anything that looked like fruit, but for their gifts in my life i do owe a word of thanks.

i have forced myself never to read too much literary theory and such. basically it annoys the fuck out of me. i have never been able to figure out what such reading projects have to do with my life — my language. i am not involved in this activity that is preoccupied with the workings of a mechanical engine to describe the beauty of the afternoon ride. this is an activity best left to the hired class.

i believe as a writer i have the right and duty to use as many writing tricks as are required to get the words into the page. as i stated above, i am comfortable using the word "dictations" to describe how i work. language floats in my head — i use it time and time again. these words, phrases, pictures, or ideas are simply what is inside me. i do not read too much meaning into them — they are what they are.

most of my work is creating from a position of compulsion. writer is a verb not a noun. but i could be wrong.

ALICE BURDICK

PHOTO: ZANE MURDOCH

Alice Burdick lives and writes poetry in First South, Nova Scotia. She is presently employed at an art gallery in Mahone Bay and as a simulated patient for the Dalhousie University Faculty of Medicine. She was born and raised in Toronto, but has also lived in Halifax, Espanola, Vancouver, and on the Sechelt Peninsula. She has been involved with the small-press scene in Canada since the early '90s. Publications include *Simple Master* (Pedlar Press), *The Human About Us* (BookThug), *Covered* (twobitter 54, Letters Press), and *Fun Venue* (The Eternal Network).

I HAVE EATEN CRUNCHY SURREAL

I have I guess a tangential relationship with surrealism. For the most part, it is a subconscious connection. When I was young I looked at books of art, visual art, that my mother had in her collection. She had a book of Swedish propaganda, collage art from the '60s and '70s, and I found the distortions, colours, and images visceral and shocking. She also did a lot of artwork related to her activism, and in these I found (and find) the combination of strong recognizable images and pure design really appealing. The trails and routes outward from the obvious are fun to follow. So the strongest influence, as far as surrealism goes, may be in this roundabout influence of visual art.

There are certain practices in surrealist writing that make sense as writing tools. The "exquisite corpse" is always surprising, with its deliberate contravention of the linear. A lot of surrealism is pretty joyful, and invites collaboration, the inclusion of many. When I think of "surrealism," I think of the early years of the 20th century, I can't help it. I picture men (yes, it's hard to picture many women in this realm, then) with waxed no-gravity moustaches tearing at their hair and writing and writing. Wait, is that Dada? The term sounds quaint. Maybe it's the handiest term to apply to work that is both accessible and confusing!

In general, the real is surreal to me. Accepted practice and behaviour take on a definitely strange hue when regarded beyond dumb acceptance. The world of structures is pretty wonky; the buildings I walk into and ride up and down; the media I gorge on that leaves me hungry in ignorance. Not to say that there is no beauty in all this. I see gorgeous things, speeding past. It's just that dreams make things clear.

KEVIN CONNOLLY

Kevin Connolly is a Toronto poet, journalist, and editor. His most recent book is *Happyland* (ECW, 2002).

I came to Surrealism first via its echoes in the contemporary poetry (most of it American) I was reading in my early twenties — James Tate, Paul Hoover, Charles Simic, Anselm Hollo. Later, the New York poets I grew to love — more obviously John Ashbery and Ron Padgett — led me to French poets they admired and translated, like Guillaume Apollinaire and the "cubist" poet Pierre Reverdy. At about that same time a friend found me a used copy of

Michael Benedikt's *The Poetry of Surrealism*, an anthology that still sits on my desk for weeks on end. It's filled with fantastic contemporary translations of all of the major surrealist writers, with the translators all excellent poets in their own right. The translations made me appreciate Eluard and Apollinaire in ways I hadn't before, and introduced me to poets largely peripheral to the movement (Hans Arp, René Daumal) who, to me, still seem far more interesting than Breton and the ever-narrowing set of standards and dictums that defined the movement proper. I followed the thread to painting, sculpture, and photography, then to Spanish and South American surrealists like Lorca, Machado, and Borges. Over the years, I've found roots and branches in surprising places — in the lines of modernist icons like Stevens and Eliot, in the distilled images of Williams and Baudelaire, or in the work of such apparently antithetical writers as W.S. Merwin and Paul Muldoon.

As a utopian social movement, Surrealism has found what is probably its proper place on history's scrap heap. Its imagery — the melting clocks, the trees made from human hands — has become the stuff of dormitory cliché. Even the word itself has been so corrupted by popular culture that "surreal" now means little more than "really weird." The hallmarks of a dead letter, you'd think. But then you leaf through Max Jacob's prose poems or Reverdy's quiet, spooky little lyrics, and they're as striking and vital as if they'd been written last week. To my mind, Surrealism's real contribution has little to do with manifestoes or morphing public tastes; it's in the works themselves, their obsession with the subconscious life of the mind. In often slapdash ways, I've employed what could broadly be described as a Surrealist method — a set of games and techniques which roadmap an escape from method (and from ego) — countless times. The approach favours vernacular over literary language, novelty over tradition, open meaning over closed meaning. It also puts randomness, surprise, invention, and discovery back into the artistic equation. Love it or hate it, a surreal poem is not about a single ego sharing thoughts and feelings in a circumscribed context, it's about finding something new and recreating the *event* that is thinking as it happens. For this writer, it has also been a saviour, especially on those nights when the need to write seems to have nothing whatever to do with having something to say.

WILLIAM A. DAVISON

William A. Davison, the world's largest sea anemone, resides in an oddly shaped attic room in downtown Toronto. He occasionally migrates downstairs to visit his partner S. Higgins, his cat, and his collection of small, black dots. His work has appeared in *Muse Apprentice Guild*, *Rampike*, and *Perpetual Motion Machine*, as well as in secret correspondences with Torpor Vigil Industries, Oneiromantic Ambiguity Collective, and the Brotherhood of the Swollen Jaw. Davison is also the founder of Recordism, an entirely new way of eating cheese.

PHOTO: S. HIGGINS

Okay, let's make one thing perfectly clear… in spite of what you may have heard, Recordism is not "an entirely new way of eating cheese." Recordism is an artistic ideology, founded by W.A. Davison in 1984, and rooted in a reevaluation of chance and automatism, the basic principles of Dada and Surrealism.

Over the years, Recordism has been developed in both theory and practice by Davison and his partner Sherri Lyn Higgins, with contributions coming in recent years from many other artists and writers associated with the International Bureau of Recordist Investigation (see www.recordism.com for more information). In his own work, Davison has applied Recordist ideas and techniques to film and video, music, performance art, installations, sculpture, painting, drawing, collage, comics, games, prose, poetry, and prose poetry.

In regards to the examples of Davison's "Recordist word art" published here, it should be noted that they are the result of a fairly pure form of automatic writing and are presented here in exactly the same manner as they were written, without editing or censoring. No claims are made to artistic merit; these works, like all Recordist works, are merely the recorded results of certain creative processes.

It is hopefully clear at this point that Recordism is not an entirely new way of eating cheese. It is instead an entirely new way of eating leftover potato salad!

BEATRIZ HAUSNER

PHOTO: SIMI ABOUTBOUL

Beatriz Hausner was born in Chile in 1958. She came to Canada with her family in 1971 where she's lived since. She has translated the works of many Latin American and European surrealists, including Eugenio Granell, Edouard Jaguer, César Moro, Olga Orozco, Ludwig Zeller, Enrique Molina, and Jorge Cáceres, many collected in the anthology *The Invisible Presence: Sixteen Poets of Spanish America* (Mosaic, 1996), others published by Oasis Publications, Canada's only surrealist press. Her first book of poems, *The Wardrobe Mistress*, was published by Ekstasis Editions in spring 2003, and the chapbook *Towards the Ideal Man Poems* was published by Lyricalmyrical Press, also in 2003.

Looking back, I would say that I became conscious of surrealism sometime around the age of nine, when Ludwig Zeller and my mother, Susana Wald, began their life together. Suddenly the walls of our small house in the neighbourhood of La Reina in Santiago, Chile, were filled with art that I now realize was surrealist, but which, at the time, seemed strange, even scary. I remember clearly a collage of Ludwig's featuring a woman's head with a huge horn growing out her ear and ending in a machine of some kind. I was both mesmerized and terrified by it. Over time, as I watched my mother and Ludwig work in their studio — a not-so-converted and extremely cold garage — I began to understand that these were other manifestations of reality.

Despite the financial difficulties of the early years of my parents' life together, difficulties I could feel, I remember our home being a lively place where artists and writers dropped by daily. These were people whose sensibility matched that of my parents', people who were themselves deeply involved in surrealism in Chile, a country with a particularly strong tradition in the movement.

We came to Canada in 1970. Susana and Ludwig, perhaps idealistically, believed they could continue their surrealist activity in Toronto, much as they had in Chile. The problem was that there were no surrealists in Toronto. None. Toronto was, in those years, completely closed to surrealism, no doubt influenced by the English-speaking world's general bias against it, its view being that surrealism is a kind of affectation, not a way of life, a way of *being* in the world. Nonetheless, Ludwig and Susana quickly established contact with galleries in the city and surrounding towns like Dundas, where they organized exhibitions for their surrealist colleagues from Europe and other parts of the world. My parents also began publishing surrealist texts, under the imprint of Oasis Publications. This is how my own involvement with surrealism began.

I was in high school. Seeing how limited the scope of my literary education was, Ludwig started exposing me to — often reading to me out loud — the poets he cherished. This is how I came to know the works of César Moro, Rosamel Del Valle, Alvaro Mutis, and many other Latin American authors associated with surrealism. Once I was in university, where I studied French literature, Ludwig steered me towards the works of the French surrealists, including contemporaries of his and Susana's who were actively publishing exquisitely illustrated books which my parents picked up in their trips to Paris or received in the mail. Yes, the mail was a true box of wonders in our house.

Many of their surrealist artist friends visited our home in Toronto. This is how I came to meet people like Edouard and Simone Jaguer, José Pierre, Arturo Schwarz, Czech surrealist Petr Kral, the Indonesian artist John Schlechter Duvall, the fabulously funny Eugenio Granell, and many others who came through our door and sat at our table. Some became and continue to be my friends.

I began translating the works of Spanish American and French surrealists sometime around the age of twenty-one or twenty-two. Getting to know the work of such wonderful poets so intimately taught me a great deal about writing and the surrealist life. The voices of Enrique Gómez-Correa, Jorge Cáceres, Aldo Pellegrini, and many of the aforementioned poets, have informed my own writing, so that my poetry speaks in cadences that grow out of that most particular and rich soil that is Latin American surrealism. It is my tradition and I carry it in my bones.

Surrealism has given me the possibility of touching the Absolute daily, here and now. The surreal exists for me totally, while walking down the streets of downtown Toronto to my job, when dancing wildly to the sounds of Sly and the Family Stone, when looking into the beloved's eyes, when watching with amazement as my daughter builds her own world. Surrealism is what I know as truth; it has never failed me.

MARK LABA

Mark Laba lives in Vancouver, where he works as the food reviewer for the *Vancouver Province* newspaper. His most recent book of poetry, *Dummy Spit*, was published by Mercury Press (2002), and before that it's anybody's guess. Numerous small press stuff from publishers like Proper Tales Press, Curvd H&z, Gesture

PHOTO: KAREN WILSON

Press, and more, along with a bunch of collaborations with the likes of Stuart Ross, jwcurry, and Clint Burnham. Novels, poetry, puppet shows, and doughnut crushing… all just part of Mark's modern lifestyle.

I'm a movie star… I feel the picture in my face… I make love with you all the time… the lights of Paris are but two quick bourbons in my itinerary… forget Wall Street… I wear the emergency pants in my family… polar chill but I like the pavement to crackle… and I've insured my ice bucket with a sea otter… late at night, snackbars and oven mitts… then Alors… Zut… gone with a wink and a handshake.

LANCE LA ROCQUE

PHOTO: LANCE LA ROCQUE

Lance La Rocque teaches "The Writer and Nature" at Acadia University in Wolfville, Nova Scotia. Currently he is studying the anatomy, psychology, and history of local flora. This work is only in the very early stages and involves the organization and gathering of samples, sketches, interviews, photographs, and records of dreams, as well as detailed research into the works of naturalist Jakob Von Uexkull. La Rocque is also working on a book exploring the relationship between nature poetry and consciousness. Most recently, he is the author of a chapbook, *The Gross Metaphysics of Meat* (Proper Tales Press).

THEREFORE: MANIFEST
I must clear the room of pencils.
I must eat cabbage in some style before every poem.
I must sharpen three to seven wooden spoons.
No plastics, no stainless steel, no more immortal utensils!
I must be sure I can see you once every three weeks
(Fridays are no good).
I will succeed at every poem, I know, if only
I can sustain the state of perfect paranoia.

Everyone is watching.
Even the objects are eyes.
Eyes off my instruments, eyes!
(At times I take a tape recorder
and ambush my organs.)
You'll have to agree, surely, by my systems, I am on the verge
of becoming a great success.

LILLIAN NECAKOV

PHOTO: ANDREW AVALOS

Over the years Lillian Necakov's work has appeared in various publications in various countries in various formats. *Hat Trick* was her last book of poetry, published in 1998 by Exile Editions. She lives and works in Toronto.

I rarely read poetry, but when I do I read Octavio Paz. My influences are cinema and collage art. These days I read mostly non-fiction, particularly books on science and mathematics. *E=mc^2: A Biography of the World's Most Famous Equation* is what you'll find on my night table.

For me the act of writing is akin to editing a film. I have all these wild images that I carry around with me and when I sit down to write I have to harness them and create a context for them. Sometimes the process is pleasurable, sometimes torturous.

As for surrealism and how it has informed my writing, I don't know, I suppose surrealism has chosen me, I have no control over that, that's just how I see the world.

STUART ROSS

PHOTO: DANA SAMUEL

Stuart Ross is a Toronto fiction writer, poet, editor, and creative-writing instructor. He has been active in the Toronto literary scene since the mid-1970s and sold 7,000 copies of his self-published poetry and fiction chapbooks (under the Proper Tales Press imprint) in the streets of Toronto during the '80s.

He has edited a bunch of literary magazines: *Mondo Hunkamooga, Who Torched Rancho Diablo?, Dwarf Puppets on Parade, Peter O'Toole,* and, most recently, the poetry journal *Syd & Shirley.* Stuart is co-founder, with Nicholas Power, of the Toronto Small Press Book Fair, an underground literary institution since 1987. He has given readings in Canada, the U.S., England, and Nicaragua.

Stuart's work has appeared in scores of journals here and in the U.S., including *Harper's, This Magazine, Geist, Rampike, sub-Terrain, Bloom Oon, WHAT!, Industrial Sabotage, Perpetual Motion Machine, Word, Fell Swoop,* and *Bomb Threat Checklist.* His poetry collections from ECW Press include *The Inspiration Cha-Cha* (1996), *Farmer Gloomy's New Hybrid* (1999), which was shortlisted for the 2000 Trillium Book Award, *Razovsky at Peace* (2001), and *Hey, Crumbling Balcony! Poems New & Selected* (ECW Press, 2003). Stuart's fiction includes *The Pig Sleeps* (a collaborative novel with Mark Laba; Contra Mundo Books, 1991), *The Mud Game* (a collaborative novel with Gary Barwin; The Mercury Press, 1995), and *Henry Kafka and Other Stories* (The Mercury Press, 1997).

His online home is www.hunkamooga.com.

Oh, the usual suspects fascinated me when I was a kid: Dali, Magritte, Hieronymous Bosch. Bugs Bunny, the Roadrunner, Felix the Cat. Hell — Dr. Seuss. Started reading some pretty weird fiction and poetry when I was a teen: Arrabal, Beckett, Joe Rosenblatt, Juan Butler, Kurt Vonnegut Jr., Hans Arp. And films: Bunuel, Jodorowsky, Herzog. I couldn't believe this stuff — this was the way the world *really* was! Maybe it was because I dreamt so rarely that I liked to explore dream states in my waking life. And being a teenage freak, an outsider with an afro on my head and tikis around my neck, I was twisted, I thrived on the offbeat. Or maybe the anti-Beat. When I discovered Ron Padgett, a second-generation New York poet, although I was already writing about people turning into lizards and stuff, it coalesced for me. And then there was Opal Louis Nations, whose work I began collecting when I was twenty and still treasure. The potential of surrealism, and the possibilities of humour in the absurd. The *humanness* of it, the humanity.

Writing is about lying, and perhaps the more extreme the lie, the better. Do I really wanna tell people about my life and that which tortures me inside my skull? There's something far more cathartic, and practical, about putting it through the mirror of distortion. Let my most sincere and heartfelt words be uttered by Mako and Sako, the twins with no skulls who appear in my novellas *Wooden Rooster* and *Guided Missiles*. "Trust the men with no skulls," they urged Carlos Venom. "Trust the men with no skulls," they urged TV viewers as U.S.-trained death squads left decapitated bodies on the sides of roads in Guatemala.

I don't strive for this skulllessness in all my writing, but it's a significant presence. The lack of skull, the absence of boundaries. The freedom to mine the should-be-possible.

STEVE VENRIGHT

Steve Venright's most recent book is *Spiral Agitator* (Coach House Books, 2000). As a visual artist, he developed variegraphy, producing psychedelic abstracts using fingerpaint and computers. As founder of Alter Sublime Neurotechnologies, he originated the Hallucinatorium, a travelling sideshow provoking illegally beautiful images in the minds of its visitors. With members of the International Bureau of Recordist Investigation, he established the TVI Mobile

PHOTO: DALE ZENTNER

Reality Inspection Lab, acclaimed for its superior on-site work and its prototypes of devices such as the Ontologator™, the Phenomenatron™, and the Vortextant™. Through Torpor Vigil Industries (www.torporvigil.com), he has released Samuel Andreyev's *Songs of Elsewhere* and an album of outrageous sleeptalks called *The Further Somniloquies of Dion McGregor*. At the demise of the 20th century, he and fellow Torpor Vigilantes attempted a nonviolent takeover of the Toronto Eaton Centre to transform it into Surreal Estate One, an ecosystem based on the visions of painter Max Ernst.

At the heart of Surrealism is revolt. The driving force behind this revolt is a longing to transform life and change the world.

When I first encountered Surrealism at age seventeen, it struck me like a bolt of neural lightning. Here was a movement that exulted in delirium, trance, dream, and desire; whose practitioners railed against anything that stood in the way of Love, Liberty, and Poetry. To a Surrealist, only the marvellous is beautiful. And the marvellous, I suddenly realized, was precisely what I was after.

Even before my introduction to Surrealist texts, I was exploring deliriomantic states of entrancement in my writing process. I tend to write, now as then, from a state of vigilant torpor, my eyes open just enough to oversee the emergence of letters onto the page. I try to find mental passageways I haven't been down before, ultimately expecting that one of them will lead right outside my mind and into some ultra-dimensional space (I thought this happened once but it turned out to be just an empty waiting room in a chiropractic clinic on Ossington Avenue). Derangement is important to me, and so is synaesthesia. My words, at their best, are psychedelic. I like Max Ernst's motto: keep one eye on the outer world and one eye focused within. Dreams are vastly underappreciated in our society. As I write this, I'm walking through a curving underground walkway at Finch Station. Rimbaud's insistence on poetry being the domain of seers has always seemed reasonable to me. When you melt it down, language is essentially a shamanic gloop out of which visions emerge and new meanings are formed. "The world is made of language," Terence McKenna said. And he was right! Like Christopher Dewdney, I'm interested in the sublime alterations that will lead to metaconsciousness. Convulsive Beauty, Black Humour, Mad Love — all this and much more has been provided by Surrealism. Through its powers, the primacy of the imagination has been restored. Leonora Carrington is responsible, through her stories and paintings, for many of Surrealism's alchemical advances. (We're living in a time of monumental corruption, ignorance, deception, and brutality.) The recorded sleeptalks of Dion McGregor — astonishing narrations from a fortuitously accessible dream realm — inspire me tremendously. My favourite Surrealist insult was perpetrated by Breton fairly late in his life when he stormed up to the podium during a Sorbonne lecture by Tzara and, in a brazen impromptu affront, drank the speaker's glass of water. I believe in domains of existence vivid and compelling beyond even this miraculous reality we call the world.

ACKNOWLEGEMENTS

TARA AZZOPARDI: "Manifesto of the Penny Arcade" and "Witness of the Penny Arcade" appeared in *Perpetual Motion Machine*. GARY BARWIN: "Shoe," "Africa," and "Charlie" appeared in *Cruelty to Fabulous Animals* (Moonstone Press, 1995); "Planting Consent" appeared in another form in *The Great Themes* (serif of nottingham editions, 2000); "Whatever-It-Was" appeared in *Writing Space Journal*; "Belonging" was commissioned by CBC Radio for the 2004 National Poetry Face-off. DANIEL F. BRADLEY: "Live Life Like in a Beer Commercial" appeared in *Daniel f. Bradley (green stag)* (Pangen Subway Ritual, 1998); "Uniform Motion Down a Staircase" appeared in *3 Poems* (BookThug, 1998); "Blind Masters" appeared as a fingerprinting inkoperated broadside (1998); "Green Ray" appeared as *Green Ray* (Pangen Subway Ritual, 1997). KEVIN CONNOLLY: "Contractual Obligation" appeared in *This Magazine*. BEATRIZ HAUSNER: "Down," "My New Bag," "Je ne mange pas de ce pain là," "Streetcar Madness," and "My Man Loss" appeared in *The Wardrobe Mistress* (Ekstasis, 2003); "Mother of Sound," "Rider," "Just Man," and "Playing House" appeared in very different form in *Towards the Ideal Man Poems* (Lyricalmyrical, 2003). LANCE LA ROCQUE: "History Is the Exception," "A Nova Scotia Love Story," "Moon:," and "Infinity" appeared in *The Gross Metaphysics of Meat* (Proper Tales Press, 2002). LILLIAN NECAKOV: "Hanging from a Telephone Wire," "Munich – Paris," and "Twelve Spirits of Chaos" appeared in *Exile*; "Fission" appeared in *Hat Trick* (Exile Editions, 1998). STUART ROSS: "The Sun" and "Sueño Perdido" appeared in *Hey, Crumbling Balcony! Poems New & Selected* (ECW Press, 2003); "Sueño Perdido" also appeared in *Razovsky at Peace* (ECW Press, 2001); "A Guy, Some Flippers, a Building" and "Experiments on Oral Suction and Gill Breathing in Five Species of Australian Tadpole" appeared in *Fell Swoop*; "A Traumatic High School Tap-Dancing Incident" appeared in *Rampike*.

THE EDITOR wishes to thank Mercury Press publisher Bev Daurio for her commitment to this project and her always-valuable guidance; Mercury's Angela Rawlings for her enthusiasm and efficiency; Dana Samuel for her unblinking support and her excellent feedback on the introduction; and, finally, the contributors to this anthology for their work, their challenges, and their suggestions.